D1737932

THE BOY'S FATHER RAN A COMPOUND FOR PRISONERS OF WAR IN ATHENS.

One day he brought home a Luger pistol.

It had been confiscated from a captured German pilot. In the boy's wide eyes it was a thing of beauty.

The year was 1941. Hitler's forces were close to conquering Greece, ushering in the years of German Occupation.

To the boy Evangelos, the Luger would come to stand for all the armed might of the Nazis. And for their fatal weakness.

Yet the road ahead held many twists and shocking surprises. Including the day when Evangelos would face the ultimate fear as he gazed point-blank into a Luger's barrel.

MY FATHER HAD THIS LUGER ... A True Story Of Hitler's Greece is an enthralling tale of the war that engulfed Europe and the world. A moving ode to the human capacity for hope and endurance, it paints a rich picture of wartime life and poignantly evokes a childhood that is as magical as it is terrifying. It is a story for today, and for all times and all ages.

Evangelos Louizos was born in Kallithea, on the outskirts of Athens, Greece, in 1933. He worked at numerous jobs, including those of sailor, bartender and construction worker, before completing his university education and becoming a teacher in the United States and Britain. He created a very successful English as a Foreign Language department at the American Community School in Cobham, Surrey. He is multilingual and passionate about human rights. An avid world traveler, he has made it a point to learn how to say Hello and Thank You in as many languages as possible.

N.J. Slabbert's Sword of Zeus Project, an initiative dedicated to Greece's experience in World War Two, proudly worked with Mr Louizos to document, research and edit his memories and present them in this true story of the war that changed the world.

German soldiers raising the flag in front of the Acropolis.

N.J SLABBERT'S
THE SWORD OF ZEUS PROJECT™
presents

MY FATHER HAD THIS LUGER...
A TRUE STORY OF HITLER'S GREECE

Evangelos Louizos

Montagu House

N.J SLABBERT'S
THE SWORD OF ZEUS PROJECT™
presents

MY FATHER HAD THIS LUGER...
A TRUE STORY OF HITLER'S GREECE

Evangelos Louizos

MONTAGU HOUSE USA

An Imprint of Truman Publishing Media Group
www.truman-news.com/Montagu_House.html
Copyright© 2012

ISBN: 978-0-9823734-3-9
Library of Congress Control Number: 2011942013

BIO006000	BIOGRAPHY & AUTOBIOGRAPHY / Historical
HIS042000	HISTORY / Europe / Greece
HIS037070	HISTORY / Modern / 20th Century
HIS027100	HISTORY / Military / World War II

N.J. Slabbert's
THE SWORD OF ZEUS PROJECT™

The Sword of Zeus Project™ is an initiative dedicated to promoting awareness, understanding and education concerning the experience of Greece and its people in World War Two. For more information please see **www.theswordofzeus.info/** or e-mail **infomontagu@gmail.com.**

Project Director: Em Saks, Managing Editor, Montagu House Publishers.

Board of Honorary Editorial Advisors:

The Hon. Aris Melissaratos (Chair), Senior Advisor to the President of Johns Hopkins University.

The Hon. Gilbert F. Decker, former Chair, U.S. Army Science Board.

Rear Admiral (Ret.) Sotirios Georgiadis, former Inspector General of the Hellenic Navy.

George Harocopos, former Greek Resistance fighter, participant with the British Special Operations Executive in the abduction of Germany's General Kreipe, author of *The Fortress Crete: The Secret War 1941-1944* and *The Forgotten Debt.*

Brigadier General (Ret.) Stergios Smirlis, former Hellenic Army General Staff Support Directorate (Land Combat and Aviation).

Mr. Jimmy Stavrakis, President, Adcor Industries.

Dr. Peter N. Yiannos, President, American Foundation for Greek Language and Culture (AFGLC) Center for Delaware, Pennsylvania and New Jersey.

Dr. Alexander Vavoulis, Professor Emeritus, California State University in Fresno, California; academic freedom leader; veteran broadcaster.

Literary and Creative Director: N.J. Slabbert.

NOTE ON NAMES AND PHOTOGRAPHS IN THIS BOOK:
All photographs in this work which carry no copyright attribution appear by permission of Evangelos Louizos, except for photographs which, to the best knowledge of the publishers, are in the public domain. Some names in this work exist in various forms and are spelled in different ways according to various sources. The spelling of some names may have changed over time and may also be subject to idiomatic and colloquial variations. The names, usages and spellings used here are those which most accurately reflect the author's memories of his area of Greece at the time of the events described in this narrative.

DEDICATION

*To Vivien, to my children
and my grandchildren*

*A special thanks to Max who
made it possible*

FOREWORD
The stories we live by
By N.J. Slabbert

My Father Had This Luger... A True Story Of Hitler's Greece is about timeless things.

While many readers will quickly see powerful connections between this tale and the dramas unfolding on the international scene in the twenty-first century, *Luger* deals with much more than conflicts between nations. It illuminates the nature of family, community and the ways in which countless minutiae give life its meaning. It tells of loyalty and sticking together, of triumph over great odds, of hope, of the universality of childhood and imagination. It reminds us of the ability of the human mind to find humor everywhere and take nourishment from it.

Luger is a product of *The Sword of Zeus Project*, a publishing initiative dedicated to Greece's part in World War Two. But this book isn't only for people of Greek background, or for those with a special interest in World War Two. It's for everyone who likes stories of remarkable experiences.

Stories are enormously important to all of us. By awakening the past for us, they help us understand the present. They entertain us by transporting us to eras and places which, though distant, are yet strangely reminiscent of our own feelings and problems. Stories of other people's journeys can help each of us to think about our own journey, who we are, what we've learned and what we dream of.

In all these ways, stories bring meaning to our lives. It's arguable that most of us find our fullest personal meaning only when we find the right story, which serves as a mirror in which we see ourselves clearly for the first time. Many people spend years searching for a story they can live by, or for a way to live their own story.

The Sword of Zeus Project was created out of the belief that there were fine stories still waiting to be told about Greece in World War Two. For millennia Greece has been an arena of great events, but in the nineteen-forties it saw heroism that was especially significant for the twentieth century and the world that arose from it.

My Father Had This Luger... A True Story Of Hitler's Greece is a deeply human tale that is quite simple on the surface but depicts complex happenings

{ 1 }

and emotions. It chronicles the war experiences of a little Greek boy, Evangelos, and movingly catches the atmosphere of war through a child's eyes. It is frightening and poignant, but also frequently funny, for children have a way of honestly seeing the comedy in adult actions even, and perhaps especially, when adults are most solemn. *Luger* also paints a warmly vivid picture of Greek community life in the second quarter of the twentieth century. Part One of the book, Golden Summer, captures especially haunting aspects of that milieu.

Producing a story based on memories of long ago is a team effort that is analogous to making a movie, for the building of a good narrative is a feat of creative architecture that calls for many skills and resources. The past has to be carefully reconstructed with scrupulous faithfulness to fact, yet a characters must be shaped into scenes. Recollections must be ordered and sculpted into the dramatic forms and nuances that storytelling demands. It is a lengthy creative process, incident by incident and sentence by sentence, involving many discussions, separate creative acts and editorial decisions. It is thus unsurprising that the development of *Luger* extended over two years, and that thanks are due for its production to many people. I will name just a few:

Evangelos Louizos, for sharing his intimate reminiscences with us and patiently cooperating in the ponderous process of developing them into an integrated story and a book.

Em Saks, Managing Editor of Montagu House Publishers, for seeing the potential of both *The Sword of Zeus Project* and *My Father Had This Luger...*, for making it possible for both to be born, for painstakingly working with Mr Louizos to document his childhood memories so that they could be developed into the story form presented in these pages, and for her remarkable historical research, storytelling judgment and editorial leadership.

Aris Melissaratos, of Johns Hopkins University, Chair of *The Sword of Zeus Project* Editorial Board, for endless encouragement and a steadfast commitment to the project's vision.

Jimmy Stavrakis and Peter Yiannos, for generously contributing practical support to the research effort underlying *The Sword of Zeus Project*.

Finally, we are all in debt to that great generation of Greece whose spirit *The Sword of Zeus Project* honors and remembers.

N.J. Slabbert
Project Creator and Literary Director
The Sword of Zeus Project

CONTENTS

PART ONE: GOLDEN SUMMER

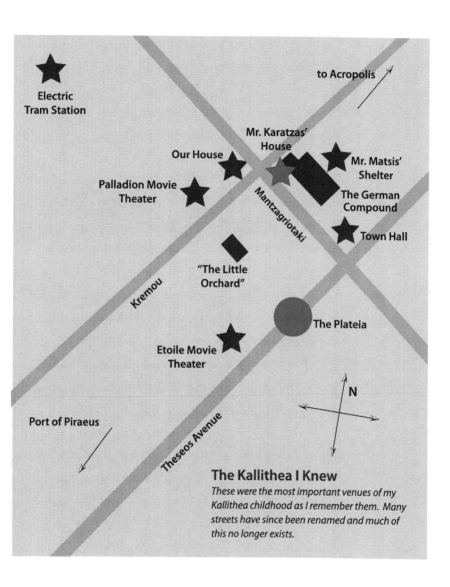

Electric
Tram Station

to Acropolis

Mr. Karatzas'
House

Our House

Mr. Matsis'
Shelter

Palladion Movie
Theater

The German
Compound

Mantzagriotaki

Town Hall

"The Little
Orchard"

Kremou

The Plateia

Etoile Movie
Theater

N

Port of Piraeus

Theseos Avenue

The Kallithea I Knew

These were the most important venues of my Kallithea childhood as I remember them. Many streets have since been renamed and much of this no longer exists.

CHAPTER 1 : THE MUSIC OF KALLITHEA

I lost my innocence when I was five years old.

Or so I assume. At any rate, Mr Karatzas, our neighbor, never again invited me to help him safely bring in the New Year.

Mr Karatzas was a man of tradition, even superstition. In December 1937 he asked my mother if I could participate in *podariko*. This is an old Greek custom which, loosely translated, means "first footing". It's believed that if the first person to enter your house on New Year's Day is good, sincere and honest, your year will be happy and prosperous. So this task is usually assigned to a child who hasn't yet been exposed to the evils of the world. The child is rewarded with candy or money.

I don't recall whether my ritual entry into his house brought Mr Karatzas especially good luck in 1938. My own luck was certainly in fine shape, since I narrowly escaped death three times that year, as I'll presently tell. Quite apart from those particular kindnesses of fate, though, I look back on that world before the war as a golden summer. When I step over Mr Karatzas' threshold in my memory, I re-enter not only his house but a milieu of Greek community life that existed once upon a time long ago, before Hitler's invaders came to call on us. The collision of that life with the darkest side of the twentieth century is the subject of this story.

And so I must begin by telling you about the warmth and wonder that was once Kallithea, before war engulfed us.

• • •

I remember that New Year's Day well.

"Off to bed with you," my mother told me the previous night. "We've an early start tomorrow."

"Why?"

"We must get up early because I have to get you ready to go to Mr Karatzas."

"Why?"

"Because you have to do *podariko.*"

"How do I do *podariko?*"

"Do nothing, just ring the bell."

Mr Karatzas was retired and had only one arm. He had lost the other in the First Balkan War, from 1912 to 1913, when Greece and a group of its allies had fought the Ottoman Empire. He lived two houses across the street from us. He was an avid fisherman. Every Sunday I watched him head for the nearby tram station, the fingers of his remaining hand firmly curled around his fishing rod. His destination was the harbor of Faliro, where his little boat lay at anchor. I was always greatly intrigued by the gloved artificial hand protruding from his deflated jacket sleeve. It reminded me of a crab claw.

"You shouldn't look at his hand," my mother admonished. I stared anyway. What child wouldn't? Mr Karatzas didn't seem to mind. He patiently explained the loss of his limb in terms I could understand. "So this is what war does to people," I mused.

• • •

Early that New Year's morning, dressed in my best, I crossed our street and climbed the five steps to ring Mr Karatzas' doorbell. The door opened and Mrs Karatzas' smiling face appeared. "Welcome, Vagelaki, come in!"

I entered, was plied with sweets and, best of all, proudly received a brand-new, shiny five-drachma coin.

It was the first and last time Mr Karatzas invited me for *podariko*. That could be taken to mean my innocence somehow expired, disqualifying me from further participation in the ceremony. If so, I wasn't alone in my loss. The civilization in which I lived was also losing a form of innocence: the fond and popular belief that we had entered an age of unprecedented rationality and civility. Contrary to this optimistic belief, Europe was moving with inexorable momentum toward a war more terrible than civilized people thought possible in the allegedly enlightened twentieth century. Within just three years those same steps up which I had just scampered, to ring Mr Karatzas' doorbell in a simple, happy ritual, would resound with the heavy tread of hobnailed boots.

They would belong to a German officer commandeering the house as his billet in the name of Adolf Hitler.

• • •

Mr and Mrs Karatzas were fixtures of the cozy, safe environment of the Kallithea in which I was born. Kallithea was then a relatively new part of Greater Athens. Its name means "beautiful view", since it is surrounded by mountains, crowned by the Parthenon and mirrored in the shimmering Saronic Gulf.

{ 9 }

Kallithea was designed in a grid. A long, wide, straight thoroughfare, Syngrou Avenue, which started at the sea and ran into the center of Athens, separated it from the district of Nea Smyrni, or New Smyrna, established by refugees who'd been expelled from Smyrna, Turkey, in 1922. About two miles west of Syngrou Avenue, and parallel with it, Kallithea was bordered by tram (electric train) tracks connecting Athens with the ancient port of Piraeus.

The Ilissos River, on whose banks Socrates had sat with his students expounding ideas that would engross the human mind for thousands of years, traversed Kallithea on its way to the sea. The river had paid its dues to time with silt and sediment. In summer it was a lazy creek but winter's long downpours turned it into an angry torrent that sometimes overflowed its banks with sad results for those who lived alongside it.

In those years there were as many empty lots as houses in Kallithea. In spring the flooded lots produced a profusion of poppies, chamomile, daisies and other wild flowers. These and the nettles were waging a vain struggle for territory against the implacable advances of building contractors, but the blossoms still covered large tracts in those years. And in the long, hot summers the air was heavy with jasmine, hyacinth, hibiscus and rose fragrances from the well-tended gardens of humble houses. Wafted by evening sea breezes, wonderful scents refreshed the people of Kallithea as the workday ended.

Another wide road, Theseos Avenue, crossed the district to link the sea with central Athens. Tram rails ran down the middle of Theseos, flanked by two wide routes for automobiles, only one of which was asphalt. Most streets in Kallithea were unpaved and few had storm drains, as the municipality couldn't afford public works. During winter rains some streets were impassable as torrents cascaded through them, further eroding unpaved sections while cleaning the paved ones to make their imperfections even more visible.

Near City Hall, Theseos Avenue looped around a central, circular plaza through which cars and trams had to pass before resuming their course. The trams did so grudgingly. Their screeching wheels as they slowed down for the circle could be heard a mile away in still summer nights.

In my memory the shrieks of those tram wheels, and all the other sounds of my Kallithea, have now become a lovely music from another time.

Great-grandfather Achileas and his daughter Smaragdi, on the island of Chios around 1918.

CHAPTER 2 : *A LITTLE PRINCE*

O ur area was dominated by the sprawling tram depot with its 1910-vintage green trams, but the real heart of Kallithea was the *plateia*, the town square.

Two refugees from Asia Minor seemed to be a permanent and indispensable part of the square. They were photographers whose long hours under the sun, seated on wicker chairs, had left them with sunburnt faces and cracked lips. Big antiquated wooden cameras perched on tripods beside them.

In the center of the plateia a splendid fountain shot jets of colored water. Lit up at night, these created a phantasmagoria of many hues.

Around the plateia little shops catered to the simple needs of the community, including cafes where elders and idlers passed the time. A couple of blocks away were two smaller squares, also surrounded by small shops that specialized in one thing or another. One of the smaller squares was paved. The other was verdant, with paths among shrubbery and benches where elders and young lovers sought serenity or privacy; the locals called it Perivolaki, Little Orchard.

At sunset the squares filled with laughing children and their mothers, grandparents and nannies.

Two of the plateia shops stood out for me. At Mr Yakoumidis' coffee-grinding shop, the whirring of a bean grinder accompanied the aroma of coffee as it permeated the area. At Mr Spyropoulos' haberdashery you could find all sorts of things, from buttons of any shape and color to yarn or multicolored thread on "Coats"-brand wooden spools, and any color dye you wished. In those days women didn't throw old dresses away but dyed them and wore them as new. Mr Spyropoulos' best-selling dye was black, a sign of the place that mourning held in our society.

Except for a rare taxi or dilapidated truck, the streets around the squares belonged to playing children. Opposite the Perivolaki was the small church of Agia Varvara, Saint Barbara, where elders came to light a candle or pray during vespers, the evening service. Byzantine chants echoed from the church, intertwining with the prayers of devout adults, the subdued discussions and gossip of the less devout, and the carefree voices of the children outside.

It was a symphony of life.

• • •

I lived a block from the church on one of the few paved streets, Mantzagriotaki, which extended from the River Ilissos to Nea Smyrni. Our modest house, Number 99, was three or four years old. It was a typical Mediterranean house with high shuttered windows and cornices around the windows and parapet. An imposing double front door of hardwood, with relief designs and brass handles, presented an ornate baroque appearance. This door had two small frosted windows with metal bars and there was a transom window above it, also with frosted glass. The house faced directly on to the street, the front door being separated from the square cement blocks of the sidewalk by three steps of terrazzo, a polished mosaic of marble and stone fragments. A metal scraper allowed you to wipe your feet before entering.

Like almost all houses in Kallithea, ours had a flat roof forming a terrace to which we climbed via a spiral of metal steps outside the house. From the terrace we were able to look out far across the Plain of Attica. Mount Hymettus dominated the northeast view through a blue haze. In keeping with the tales of Greek gods that formed the backdrop of our culture, I liked to see this great mountain as a reclining, half-naked giant wearing a small grove of pine trees on his midriff. This image was consistent with the myth and story of our landscape. For example, Mount Aegaleo, which blocked our view to the west, was the vantage point from which, some two and a half thousand years earlier, King Xerxes I of Persia had witnessed his fleet's destruction at the Battle of Salamis.

Farther north Mount Parnitha and Mount Penteli towered. These had yielded the marble to build the Parthenon, the majestic temple that presided over all Athens from the citadel of the Acropolis, sacred to all Greeks and venerated by the world as a beacon of civilization. Even at our considerable distance we could see the gashes inflicted on Mount Penteli's slopes by marble quarriers since antiquity.

In the center of Athens stood Lycabettus Hill, or Wolf Hill, topped by the small white church of Saint George and a cannon that was fired on special occasions. About a mile south of the hill the Parthenon brooded in its timeless dreams.

A little farther south, on Philopappou Hill, a marble Roman monument from the centuries of the Caesars marked Kallithea's northern perimeter. Beyond that point the expanse of our district unfolded toward the blue waters of the Aegean.

This was where I had my childhood, wrapped in horizons of history farther than the human eye could see.

• • •

A golden thread running through my story is the sense of heritage and family lore that pervaded our lives. We were held together by a profound awareness of our collective identity and of our obligations not only to each other but to our colorful forebears.

My maternal grandmother, Alexandra Kouvara, whose children were my mother and my Uncle Alfredos, was known to me as Yaya. She was born on the island of Tinos around 1875 to a large impoverished family which later moved to Athens. She lived in a small house on Skoufa Street where she struggled to make a living as a seamstress. On the same street lived Mr Athanasios Theodorakopoulos, a cloth merchant and widower with a daughter, Mary.

Athanasios fell in love with Alexandra Kouvara but his love went unrequited. One day he decided he had waited long enough. He hired a horse-drawn coach, stopped outside Alexandra Kouvara's house and rapped on the door. When she appeared he produced a pistol and said, "If you don't marry me, I will kill you and kill myself".

How could she refuse?

• • •

My paternal great-great-grandfather Evangelos was from the island of Chios and must have been born around the time of the French Revolution in the 1790s. He is said to have been a giant of a man, and the following story about him has been handed down through the generations:

In 1821, communities of Greeks rose up in revolt against the Turkish Ottoman Empire that had ruled them for hundreds of years. These clashes spread to Chios and in 1822 Ottoman ships, filled with soldiers, bore down on the island and a massacre of some twenty thousand Greeks ensued.

My great-great-grandfather Evangelos had a citrus orchard on the island. When the slaughter began, he and his pregnant wife, whose name has been lost to me, split up to try to increase their individual chances of survival. A kind and courageous Turkish neighbor hid Evangelos in his cellar. My great-great-grandmother fled to the mountains where, alone, she gave birth to a boy named Achileas.

Meanwhile crowds of Ottoman soldiers had assembled around fires on Chios to relax with an accustomed entertainment: wrestling matches. Among the grunting, oiled contestants was a huge, apparently invincible Turkish wrestler who had beaten hundreds of challengers. The kind Turk who had hidden great-great-grandfather Evangelos watched until he could not resist blurting out to the Turkish commander, "I know a man who can beat this champion. But you must swear to me that no matter what, you won't harm him." The intrigued commander wasn't one to be denied the pleasure of a spectacular wrestling match, and agreed. The challenger was fetched.

He was my great-great grandfather. He not only beat the Turk but broke his arm.

When the commander learned that the winner was a Greek, he reneged on his promise and the crowd rushed forward to lynch Evangelos. Fortunately, at that very minute, there was a tremendous explosion. A tiny Greek fleet from the island of Psara had slipped into the harbor unseen and had attached a fire ship to the Turkish flagship, causing its powder to explode. About two thousand Turks were killed, included the Ottoman admiral. In the confusion Evangelos escaped.

His son, Achileas, fathered five children. One was my grandfather, who also bore the name Evangelos. As is traditional in Greece, my grandfather's name was passed to me.

My father was born in Galati, Romania, at the end of the nineteenth century. After his mother's death he was taken to Chios, then still under the rule of the Ottomans, to be raised by his Aunt Smaragdi. He told me of the rejoicing when, in 1912, Chios became part of Greece. At eighteen he became a law student in Athens, where he and my mother met and fell in love. But a telegram arrived with the news that his father had died of a stroke at fifty-seven, leaving a successful business that exported citrus fruit all over northern Europe.

But the year was 1917. World War One was under way and my father was drafted, preventing him from succeeding his father immediately. As a second lieutenant he served in Macedonia, in Asia Minor and in the Greek Expeditionary Force that fought the Bolsheviks in Ukraine. When the war ended he returned to Athens, married my mother and went to Catania, Sicily, join the family business that was based there. They lived in a palatial home on the most exclusive street. My sisters were born there.

In 1922 the fascist leader Mussolini came to power in Italy. To rid the country of foreigners he made it very difficult if not impossible for them to do business in Italy. My father was compelled to join the Fascist Party and get an identity card. In 1932 his property was confiscated. The family moved to Greece, where my father took a new career as an accountant for an insurance company. And it was in Greece that I was born.

For centuries, therefore, our family's adventure had been the adventure of Greece itself, as was the case with countless other Greek households. No illustrious royal house ever handed down its chronicles with greater pride than that with which every Greek family told its ancestral story. Those who wished to conquer Greece would find a nation in which every family was a little royal house on its own, fiercely devoted to the honor and survival of its line.

In my own family, I was the youngest, and I was the male who would be responsible for perpetuating our name and continuing our rich lineage.

No wonder, then, that I was treated like a little prince.

CHAPTER 3 : STREET OPERA

In my mother's eyes I was like the owl child in an old Greek fable. Mrs Partridge, the fable goes, asked her friend Mrs Owl to deliver some food to her child at school, explaining that she would spot the little one easily because it was clearly the most beautiful child in the school. But Mrs Owl returned with the food undelivered. She couldn't find any child at the school lovelier than her own.

My mother was similarly certain that I was beautiful beyond compare. When I was a few months old she had me professionally photographed in a pose recalling Goya's famous painting The Naked Maja. In 1936 she entered me in a "most beautiful child" contest. My photo won first prize. I still have the brittle, yellowed newspaper clipping as well as the original photo, on which she wrote: "And this is my one and only boy at the age of 3. Kallithea 25 September 1936."

My mother's name was Anna but everyone called her by its diminutive, Nina. My father was Niko for Nikolaos, but to me he was Baba. I had three older sisters: Maria by twelve years, Alexandra (named after our grandmother) by ten, Evangelia (Litsa) by five.

My earliest awareness was of a loving environment, and my mythic imagination soon found a symbol of the immense benevolence that I felt focused upon me. The first thing I saw when I looked out my window every morning was a eucalyptus tree at the house of our neighbor Mrs Karaveris. My fancy turned this ever-familiar tree into a person and a friend. On windy winter days its swaying limbs became a wise patriarch's fingers wagging to remind my mother to dress me warmly. In summer I saw the branches dance happily in gentle sea breezes, inviting me to go out and play. The tree was a devoted, constant listener to whom I confided my childish secrets.

My tree, for I thought of it as mine, was my quietest companion. My family was lively. For one thing, we were musical. My sisters Maria and Alexandra played the violin. The whole family sang together every day. In time I joined them. Strauss, Lehár, Offenbach, Italian ballads and modern Greek songs resonated through our house. Music of one kind and another abounded all around us.

Beyond our family was our community, and the street songs were its anthems. To understand the world we inhabited in Kallithea before the war, you have to close your eyes and hear the street songs.

• • •

The streets of Kallithea in those days rang with the cries of vendors hoping to coax the neighborhood ladies out of their houses with bags and baskets ready to be filled. As these hawkers extolled the virtues of their goods we didn't have to listen to their words to know what they were selling. Their voices were enough: the melodic fluctuations, the rise and fall of their chants, the rhythm with which their often incomprehensible words were sung.

Some vendors carried their wares; some had donkey carts; others trundled pushcarts.

The fisherman, an unshaven old man with gray hair and a big moustache, balanced on his head a large wicker basket inlaid with blue linoleum. He sang *"The fishermaaaaaan!"* with such tempo and enthusiasm that it sounded like the beginning of a military march.

The vegetable man, his cart pulled by a sad donkey, loudly itemized his produce to one and all but you nevertheless had to look in his cart to see what he had that day, because no one could make out what he was yelling except for the last item he mentioned. This final offering alone was invariably articulated with such power and brio that it sounded like Ridi, Pagliaccio, the aria from Leoncavallo's opera Pagliacci, except that his lyric was, *"...and fresh tomatooes!"* In winter this became, *"...and fresh caaaaabbage!"*.

An old woman, hunched after spending who knows how long collecting greens from the fields, howled shrilly, *"The greeeeeeeeeeeeeeens woman!"* Her look and sound reinforced my images of the witches in the fairy tales my sisters told me.

The collier, atop a cart drawn by a skinny horse, had black clothes and a black face that made the whites of his eyes shine even in daylight. His cry, *"The coooooahllier!"*, sounded like a joyful tavern song that invited you to enjoy some good company with food and drink, but like the fisherman's tantalizingly unfinished march it left you thirsting for more.

Then there was the mattress man. On his shoulder he carried a strange tool, like a musical instrument, which made your cotton mattresses fluffy again.

There was the wicker man who repaired your chairs. The man who sharpened your knives and scissors. The milkman, Mr Mitros. The Gypsy women in their colorful dresses who exchanged empty bottles for clothespins and read your palm. The newspaper man boisterously enumerating his publications.

For me, the sweetest voice of all was the ice cream man's. Tall and smiling, he pumped a tricycle with a big white box on it. At his sound

I rushed out, coin in hand, to buy a small ice cream cone.

He was patient with my questions.

"Why's there steam coming out of the box?"

"It's not steam, it is dry ice."

"But ice is wet."

• • •

In the orchestra of our neighborhood the vendors' horses and donkeys played their parts, braying and neighing. Sometimes I'd add to their variety of sounds. Approaching the snout of one of these beasts as close as I dared, I'd stick my tongue out and blow a raspberry. Inevitably the animal erupted in a sneeze-like snort.

If music is an apt metaphor for the multifarious community life of Kallithea on the eve of World War Two, opera, or at least operetta, is at least as valid an image. Our street was made up of familiar patterns of dialogue, little comedies and dramas replayed with comforting regularity and witty ripostes.

"Is the fish fresh?"

"Fresh? Madam, the poor thing was swimming in the sea this morning until I caught it. You're insulting me now. Have I ever sold you anything that wasn't fresh?"

"Aren't they a little expensive?"

"With all respect, Madam! Go to the market and see for yourself the prices they charge over there. As it is I'm almost giving them away free."

"Is the watermelon sweet?"

"Missus, I'll cut it right now for you and if it isn't as sweet as honey I'll eat it all myself, in front of you! Please, Madam. Don't squeeze those. They're fruit, not a car's horn. How am I going to sell them if you do that?"

Every neighborhood had its own bakery, greengrocer and grocery store with its loyal clientele. These and the street vendors supplied the ingredients that made magic smells emanate from innumerable kitchens. We could often guess what our neighbors were having for dinner.

In our family the master chefs were my mother and grandmother. Despite my fussy eating habits I could never resist what they prepared. Our Sundays were always special. Thanks to my grandmother, a candle burned before the icons of saints and incense filled the air. At noon we all sat around the table for the meal. And in that golden summer before the war, although meat was a rarity during during the week we could always look forward to it on Sundays.

• • •

The street shows included, of course, seasonal ones. Every Christmas, soon after dawn, the children came to "tell" the Christmas carols, holding little metal triangles which they hit with a metal rod. The word "tell", used in Greece to describe carol-singing, refers to the ritual rhyming exchange between children and householders before the singing. The children rang the doorbell and when the lady of the house appeared they asked: "Shall we tell them, Lady?" (*Na ta poume, Kyra?*)

Tradition encouraged her to reply: "Tell them, tell them." (*Peste ta, peste ta.*)

The carolers rang their triangles and sang: "Christ is born today in the town of Bethlehem ..."

And so on.

On rare occasions, if the householder had had enough after the umpteenth carolers' visit, the exchange went differently.

"Shall we tell them, Lady?"

"Others have told them." (*Ta ipan alli.*)

If the children heard this unwelcoming statement, their standard reply was: "Let the parrots eat you, then." (*Na sas fan I papagali.*) They departed to "tell" the carols to others.

And so the neighborhood resonated with the sounds of ringing triangles and the voices of happy children collecting pennies.

• • •

The Gypsies lived northwest of Kallithea at a place called Three Bridges. Twice a year, during the February carnival and on May Day, they had a monopoly on entertainment in Kallithea. But at Christmas they came only at night, perhaps because they felt they couldn't compete with the children who came caroling earlier.

The Gypsies didn't sing their carols. Instead they employed the technology of 1915. They worked in pairs. One held a decrepit phonograph with a big horn. The other placed the needle on a record so old and overused it sounded like a chorus of dying people who could barely breathe. Sometimes the phonograph itself died. As its operator wound it frantically to keep the music going, the needle jumped, ending the show prematurely, a finale often welcomed by the long-suffering audience.

On May Day I remember four or five Gypsies doing the rounds in makeshift costumes. Since tradition associated horses with the welcoming of spring, they had fashioned a horse out of papier-mâché on a wooden frame, like an oversized piñata. They bore it aloft, fastened to their shoulders with straps. One of them, wearing traditional Greek costume, danced inside this contrivance while the others rang doorbells and collected money.

To the adults the horse might have looked like a monstrous version of the Trojan Horse but to me it was enchanting and recalled Bucephalus, the fabled horse of the great Greek ruler Alexander the Great. I watched agog as the Gypsy within the horse pirouetted.

On May Day the Gypsies also regaled us with Gaitanaki, the Greek folk dance. Dressed as women, with painted lips and rouged cheeks, they stuck a beribboned Maypole on an empty lot and danced around it, intertwining the dangling ribbons.

It has all stayed etched in my memory across the generations. It may not have been great performance art, but it was part of the color, pageantry and lifeblood of the Kallithea of my childhood, and of who we were in those days before the war.

CHAPTER 4 : *THE QUIET EVENINGS*

In many cases I wasn't the intended audience of the music of our neighborhood. Capitalizing on the invisibility of children, I learned much by quietly eavesdropping on the grown-up world around me. I continued this practice throughout my childhood. Numerous memories described in this book stem from what I overheard. Sometimes by chance, sometimes by stealth.

While my sisters did their schoolwork I sat with them, hands under my chin, listening intently as they discussed The Third Republic, morganatic weddings, Prussians and Russians (the two always sounded the same to me).

Listening to the neighborhood's older boys inevitably expanded my vocabulary. One day the whole family was sitting at the dinner table when I suddenly asked: "What are pubic crabs?"

Conversation ceased. Deathly silence ensued. The adults exchanged looks.

"Where did you hear that?" my mother asked icily.

I explained that Vergiris, a boy who lived around the corner, had seen a man on the beach scratch himself inside his bathing suit until he found a pubic crab.

The subject was changed without any satisfactory explanation.

Another time I asked my mother for permission to accompany the older children on an expedition. When pressed I divulged that its purpose was to visit the stables across the river to watch the bull mount the cow.

I was kept inside the house the rest of the afternoon.

Other times I learned from my grandmother. Elders were revered in our world, and my grandmother possessed a special authority as a source of both wisdom and knowledge. When she sewed on our Singer sewing machine I was in charge of passing the thread through the needle because Yaya (an affectionate Greek name for a grandmother) couldn't see well. And while she worked, she talked.

Oh, how she talked.

She talked about the Kaiser of Germany. She talked about the great influenza epidemic of 1918. She talked about the assassination of the King of Yugoslavia. All the great events of the world seemed to have passed through my grandmother's brain and it all came out through her lips while she sewed. I heard it all.

Some of the time she talked to me; at other times she mused rhetorically about things that interested her and it was almost as if I were present by accident.

Her favorite subject for a long time was the big social event of that decade: Britain's monarch had abdicated to marry an American socialite.

"Can you imagine Edward giving up a kingdom for that Wallis Simpson? What did he find in her?" She shook her head, gave the sewing machine a power burst and continued to another subject as though she considered the shocking abdication unworthy of further attention.

But I always knew it was not the last I would hear of Mrs Simpson.

• • •

The pattern of our neighborhood life was built on friendships. My parents and sisters had rich lives in this regard, while I explored the neighborhood accompanied by friends whose names are with me to this day: Kyriakos, whom we all called Boubi, Themos, Andreas, and others. At that age they were mostly boys, although a few little girls like Georgia and Lilika were allowed to join us when our war games required a helpless heroine to protect.

Occasionally we were joined by other children from a few blocks away. But we were territorial at heart. Boys with whom we played peacefully on Monday were ruthlessly expelled on Tuesday with the stones that were so amply supplied by the unpaved streets of Kallithea.

Movies shaped our games. Our cinemas were the Etoile, the Krystal and, a block from our house, the Palladion, an open-air, summer-only cinema that occasionally hosted live entertainers. We sat among planters with flowers. Jasmine perfumed the air. People in adjoining houses enjoyed free entertainment from their terraces.

It's hard to convey the impact during the nineteen-thirties of those gigantic movie screens and their dazzling wonders. To us in Kallithea, Hollywood was as exotic as Mars. The old silent movie *Son of the Sheik*, with Rudolph Valentino, turned me into the Sheik. The silent movie *Birth of a Nation*, about the American Civil War, featured a famous scene where a soldier rammed the flag of the Southern army into the barrel of a Northern cannon. Inspired, I stuck a broomstick into our neighbor's drainpipe, bending it out of shape.

My sisters collected movie star photos which they spread over the floor to admire: Clark Gable, Robert Taylor, Spencer Tracy, Myrna Loy, Franchot Tone, Wallace Beery, Charles Boyer, Danielle Darrieux, Zarah Leander, Marlene Dietrich. They liked to make comments that showed off their knowledge of this glamorous world. "Jean Harlow died from uremia."

And the movies added, too, to the music that was Kallithea. The musicals of Deanna Durbin, Jeanette MacDonald and Nelson Eddy encouraged my sister Maria, who had an exceptionally good voice, to sing show tunes, and the whole family joined in harmony.

• • •

On the other hand, the movies had a hand in one of my three near-death experiences of 1938.

After seeing the Norwegian Olympic ice skating champion Sonja Henie on the screen I was delighted to discover, at a construction site, a patch of ground with a glossy, smooth white surface. With visions of myself sliding along as beautifully as Miss Henie, I jumped on to what I perceived to be a solid surface. I immediately sank up to my knees: it was a caustic lime pit. My playmate shot off for help. Managing to crawl out and stagger homeward, I approached Mr Karatzas' house to find about fifteen people running toward me, having abandoned their Easter lamb roast in the garden. By the time my wounds were treated the roast was not quite the same.

Two other brushes with death, however, were triggered not by Hollywood but by my discovery of Greek legends. After learning that Icarus had sought to fly with home-made wings, I leaped from the terrace of a house under construction, flapping my arms. That might easily have been the end of me, but I landed on a pile of sand and just sprained my foot. I couldn't walk for a week.

Then my sister Alexandra told me of Prometheus, who'd stolen fire from Zeus and given it to humankind. Being a descendent of the ancient Greeks who had received this gift, I decided it was only logical that I should be a master of fire, so I poured rubbing alcohol on my feet and set them alight. My screams summoned the whole family. I was rushed to the clinic.

• • •

The steady rhythm of our family life in Kallithea before the war was thus disturbed by a single note of disorder: me. I couldn't keep out of trouble. After learning about explorers I crawled through an open manhole to explore a sewer. I came out smelling like a skunk and had to be hosed down outside the house before being given a bath. My unruly behavior upset family and neighbors. Everyone complained to my parents. My sisters had to go to Mr Kardamitsis' pharmacy regularly for alcohol, iodine and hydrogen peroxide to dress the wounds that my adventures routinely inflicted on me. It transpired that I had a genius for seeking out danger and tempting fate.

And yet I knew that whatever happened, at the end of the day I would go home and all would be well. Our lives rested upon the quiet evenings in which the family came together, as did the families of our friends and neighbors. Our home was the ultimate place of security, as it had always been and always would be.

How unbelievably sweet and innocent it all now seems.

The Führer, Adolf Hitler.

CHAPTER 5 : THE GREAT MIRACLE

One day the music of our household acquired a whole new dimension. My father brought home a radio.

This may seem a trivial purchase to the modern reader, but for us it was momentous. It was the first time I had encountered such a device. Its magnitude was shown by the fact that a technician accompanied my father to install it with the air of a learned surgeon.

It was a table model made of beautifully polished, chestnut-colored wood. The technician spent some time connecting the wires, drilling holes through the window frame and setting up a big aerial on the terrace.

We were spellbound.

We gathered about this technological wonder every day to listen raptly to what it brought us from the wide world beyond Kallithea. We called it *Er-Ce-Ah*: the French pronunciation of the letters RCA. None of us spoke English: only Greek, Italian and French.

In the lower middle of the polished cabinet's brown façade was a big pointer in a round dial displaying exotic names like *Grenoble, Luxembourg, Bratislava, Gratz, Schenectady, Rome, London, Budapest, Berlin.* I was amazed to see how just a turn of the dial magically connected us to these faraway places via a brown cloth-covered speaker overlaid by an elaborate wooden scroll.

Although our lives had always been filled with music, this was different. Not only Greek songs but *Funiculì, Funiculà,* Strauss waltzes and the *Berliner Luft* march were now coming to us from other corners of our own country, as well as from the great cities of Europe and the world.

We were all delighted, and we sang along. The radio was truly a Great Miracle of technology that put us in touch with the rest of the world in a way that I regarded as almost magical.

But the radio also brought us something very different from joyous music. Out of it came news programs that drastically affected our household atmosphere. These daily broadcasts were of course incomprehensible to me, but children are sensitive to moods and I was quick to detect the change that came over my parents when, after the news bulletins, they conversed in low tones between themselves and with our neighbors. I noticed, too that in these solemn discussions some words were repeated more than others: Czechoslovakia, mobilization, Sudetenland, Germans, Daladier, Chamberlain, Munich.

Hitler.

• • •

All this found its way into my Yaya's sewing talk. She now muttered of Neville Chamberlain, the Prime Minister of England, with his ubiquitous umbrella as we saw him in the newsreels at our weekly movie.

"Oh, that silly man! Why is he carrying an umbrella all the time if it's not raining?" The burst of the sewing machine would drown her additional comments about him and his Munich Conference.

• • •

Looking back, it seems to me now that the coming of the radio into our home marked the winding-down of an old order of life. We had seen foreign statesmen posturing in the newsreels at the movies but on those occasions there had always been a sense that such people and their doings were, in a way, as remote from our lives as the Hollywood features that followed.

By contrast, the radio brought them for the first time into our midst.

Hitler's ominous rants could now shatter the peace of any household that possessed one of those miraculous RCA cabinets. You had the option of switching the thing off, but Europe was then entering a time when the silence of unknowing was even more sinister than the thunderous oratory of the madman in Berlin. And so the projection of his awful voice into our formerly insular family life was not simply a noise that could be switched off. It portended this sinister man's power to extend his fist throughout our continent.

In more ways than one, the music of Kallithea was being steadily overshadowed by the crescendo building up in Berlin.

• • •

Autumn, 1938, brought the customary seasonal transformation of our home. Persian carpets and runners were taken out of storage, hung out for a while to get rid of the smell of mothballs, then laid down in preparation for the series of ceremonial days that marked the advent of winter. These included Saint Nicholas Day, December 6, which was especially important to us because it was my father's Name Day, the day celebrating the saint whose name he bore.

It was a day steeped in ritual. The same guests came every year. I received the customary comments and questions.

"How much you've grown!"

"Are you a good boy?"

"When are you going to school?"

Amid these time-honored exchanges I suppose that even on a feast day my elders must have discussed the growing turmoil of Europe, taking care that such conversation took place while small ears like mine were out of the room.

• • •

Christmas came. Kalanda – carols – were once more presented by the children with their metal triangles, and by the Gypsies with the same old phonograph and the worn-out record with the sore throat.

My family gave a Christmas party. My mother and sisters prepared a feast and the dining room furniture was moved against the wall to make room for dancing. Everyone had a splendid time. I sat in a corner delighting in the whole scene. Mr Archimandritis, the police chief, told jokes. Our friend Mr Matsis' big stomach bounced up and down as he clumsily danced the Lambeth Walk.

On New Year's Eve the whole family gathered around the table to play games for pennies supplied by parents. When the clock struck midnight everyone received a small drink of brandy to toast the New Year, even small children who could have only a taste.

Despite the winter cold we opened the dining room window and listened. Every ship that was docked in the nearby port of Piraeus blew its whistle. The joyful sounds reverberated throughout Kallithea.

We cut the Vasilopita, the Pie of Saint Basil, a big, sweet cake resembling a large French brioche in which a coin was hidden. A piece was cut for everyone present as well as for absent loved ones.

My father cut the cake, proclaiming, "The first piece is for our home ...the second piece is for ...," and so on, until a piece had been allotted to every member of the family, present and absent. Whoever got the piece containing the coin would be heartily congratulated, for they would have good fortune in the coming year.

I didn't find the coin that evening. But I didn't need it. Nor was I troubled that Mr Karatzas had not again thought me innocent enough to want me for *podariko*.

Despite the apprehension with which my elders awaited 1939, I remained well pleased with the music that was Kallithea in that golden summer. To me, life was perfect.

PART TWO : THE STORM BREAKS

*Evangelos in his fascist uniform at the Olympic Stadium,
pensively awaiting the arrival of the King.*

CHAPTER 6 : *I SNUB THE KING*

In 1939 I became a child mascot of a fascist organization. I was also extremely rude to the King of Greece.

But let me begin with New Year's morning.

In most of the Christian world, tradition holds that Saint Nicholas, also known as Santa Clause, fills children's stockings with presents on Christmas Eve. Greece has a different tradition: Saint Basil fills their shoes with gifts on New Year's Day. So on New Year's morning, 1939, I rushed to find my gifts. But one present was handed to me directly by my godmother, Maritsa. "This," she said, kissing me, "is something that'll help you get to know the world."

The gift couldn't have been more eerily symbolic of that fateful year, in which the fortunes of all of Europe's peoples were to be interwoven as never before. It was a game in which each player received a map of a different part of Europe. There were buttons, each marked with a city's name. You picked a button and called out the city. To win you had to be first to cover every city on your map. This was the dawn of my reading: I learned to associate the spoken names of cities with their printed names.

When I was alone I spread the maps on the dining room table. Moving a stick over them, I imagined myself flying all over Europe in a biplane of the sort I'd seen in movies and books. I memorized the names of places on the maps. Some would soon have their borders altered forever.

Some would just disappear.

• • •

Spring came to Kallithea. My friends and I caught butterflies, lady-birds and shiny flying green scarabs that we tied on strings.

Our *Er-Ce-Ah* radio's repertoire of music provided a happy distraction from news bulletins which now depressed the adults even more. Phrases like *Polish Corridor* and *Mussolini's invasion of Albania* peppered the broadcasts and the endless conversations that they triggered. It wasn't necessary to understand any of it to feel the mounting uncertainty and fear.

Not that fear was unknown in Greece. I've mentioned my great-great-grandfather's escape during the massacre on the island of Chios under the Ottoman Empire. I've also spoken of our neighbor Mr Karatzas' loss of an arm in the Balkan War of 1912-1913. These brief references speak to the fact that despite the tranquility of my childhood neighborhood, Greeks had a tempestuous history, filled with political upheaval and strife. The winds of dictatorship that blew across Europe in the twenties and thirties, creating dictatorships in Germany, Italy and Spain, didn't spare Greece. By 1939 we'd been living under a dictatorship for years. On August 4, 1936, a Greek general, Ioannis Metaxas, had set himself up as a dictator with the approval of our King, George II. As Mussolini was called *Il Duce* and Hitler *Führer,* Metaxas chose to be called *Kyvernitis.* These titles all meant "leader" in one way or another. Some Greeks welcomed dictatorship as a possible solution to the social instability and economic depression of the times. Metaxas promised prosperity and protection from Bolshevism (revolutionary communism), among other things. But Greeks paid a high price for these hopes. The Press was muzzled, dissidents were imprisoned or exiled and a secret police force was established. Not everyone was happy. My mother had long discussions with Mr Mitros, our milkman, who supported Bolshevism. In my growing role as a skilled eavesdropper I heard street vendors agreeing with him in wholehearted but hushed tones.

Taking their cue from Mussolini and Hitler, the Greek fascists established a National Youth Organization called EON. Younger members were called Pioneers, older ones Phalangists. I was too young to join but in 1939 my mother, ever eager to see me in the limelight, managed to have me made an official EON mascot. A splendid uniform was tailored for me, with a Sam Browne belt and boots crafted by Antonis the cobbler. I became a tiny fascist icon. EON supporters paraded through Athens with me at their head, in my regalia. Applauding crowds lined the streets. I must have looked like a little wind-up marching toy. At the Olympic Stadium my mother and I were placed near seats reserved for King George II and the future king and queen, Prince Paul I and his wife Frederica of Hanover. I was told that when the royals appeared I must click my heels smartly and give the fascist salute. I stood at attention and waited, beaming, until an ill-briefed official shooed me away. Tears were shed. Someone explained the arrangements to the official, who tried to make amends and return me to my post, but it was too late; my pride was hurt and I refused. When the royal party arrived and took their seats on their fancy cushions, the King spotted me in my glorious uniform and beckoned. Again I refused. Even a royal edict couldn't make me change my mind. My frantic mother promised me any kind of chocolate my heart desired if only I'd go to the King. I still refused. His Majesty tried one more time, then ignored me for the rest of the celebration.

Later, at a fascist celebration at Kallithea's Etoile movie theater, I was more accommodating. I gave the fascist salute to EON's founder, Alexandros Kanellopoulos, who held me in his arms and kissed me. This scene was caught in a photograph which I still have.

But I never got another opportunity to be photographed with the King.

• • •

One day a contraption was installed on the roof of the City Hall, four blocks down the street from our house. The new device was black, sat on four sturdy legs and had a conical top. It reminded me of the Chinese with funny hats I'd seen in books, so I called it "The Chinaman".

"What is it, Mama?" I asked.

"It's an air raid siren."

"What does it do?"

"It wails very loudly to warn people when airplanes come to drop bombs on them."

"Why should they do that?" I asked

"Because there may be war."

"Why should there be war, mama?" I persisted. My mother looked at me sadly. Her eyes became moist, her tone gruffer.

"Go wash your hands and come eat."

I made a mental note to ask others about this.

One evening we had our first air raid exercise. Adults waited nervously, glancing at the clock and speaking in low voices. Then a piercing, undulating wail burst forth, flowing across the whole district. It sent chills down my spine.

On another evening I accompanied my mother to an obligatory air defense class for ladies. It was held in an elementary school classroom.

"This," Mama told me, "is going to be your school in September."

I looked around with short-lived curiosity. My first experience in my future school was one of utter tedium. In the middle of the umpteenth demonstration on how to assemble and disassemble a gas mask, I decided I'd had enough. I jumped up and yelled at the top of my lungs. I screamed and screamed until I ran out of breath, then sat down and crossed my arms, satisfied with my impact. The startled lecturer, a policeman, dropped his mask. Women leaped up. Some, perhaps thinking the war had started, looked as if they might faint. Children began crying. Embarrassed, Mama got up and took me home. It was the first of many times my disruptive powers were to be exercised under that roof.

• • •

On Sunday evenings in summer our family went to the movies. In late August that year we saw an exciting American film at the Krystal cinema. Police and gangsters killed each other mercilessly. Wild automobile pursuits ended up in crashes from which people somehow emerged unscathed. The hero somehow got himself into a situation in which he was precariously perched on a stepladder leaning against a two-story building. The villain was on the roof shoving the ladder, which teetered back and forth, back and forth. Suddenly, the house lights came on. To my deep disappointment I learned I had to wait a week to see the rest of the story, for serials were shown at the movies in those days, with cliffhanger endings designed to bring the audiences back. On our way home I made Mama promise that we'd return the next weekend to discover the outcome.

Alas, we didn't. On the following Sunday, September 3, 1939, our *Er-Ce-Ah* brought news that overshadowed all else. At 11:15 in Britain that morning, Britain's Prime Minister, Neville Chamberlain, gave a speech on BBC Radio. To those who are familiar with this speech from time-worn recordings, it is a relic of the distant past.

To me, and to the Greece that I describe in this book, it was the life-changing event that the adults in my life had dreaded. This is what Chamberlain's very precise voice said:

I am speaking to you from the Cabinet Room at 10 Downing Street. This morning the British Ambassador in Berlin handed the German Government a final note stating that unless we heard from them by 11.00 a.m. that they were prepared at once to withdraw their troops from Poland, a state of war would exist between us. I have to tell you that no such undertaking has been received, and that consequently this country is at war with Germany. You can imagine what a bitter blow it is to me that all my long struggle to win peace has failed. Yet I cannot believe that there is anything more or anything different I could have done and that would have been more successful. Up to the very last it would have been quite possible to have arranged a peaceful and honorable settlement between Germany and Poland, but Hitler would not have it.

He had evidently made up his mind to attack Poland whatever happened; and although he now says he has put forward reasonable proposals which were rejected by the Poles, that is not a true statement.
The proposals were never shown to the Poles nor to us; and although they were announced in a German broadcast on Thursday night, Hitler did not wait to make comment on them, but ordered his troops to cross the Polish frontier.

His actions show convincingly that there is no chance of expecting that this man will ever give up his practice of using force to gain his will. He can only be stopped by force.

We and France are today, in fulfillment of our obligations, going to the aid of Poland, who is so bravely resisting this wicked and unprovoked attack on her people. We have a clear conscience. We have done all that any country could do to establish peace. *The situation in which no word given to Germany's ruler could be trusted and no people or country could feel themselves safe has become intolerable.*

And now that we have resolved to finish it, I know that you will play your part with calmness and courage.

At such a moment as this the assurances of support that we have received from the Empire are a source of profound encouragement to us. When I have finished speaking certain detailed announcements will be made on behalf of the Government. Give these your closest attention.

The Government have made plans under which it will be possible to carry on the work of the nation in the days of stress and strain that may be ahead. But these plans need your help.

You may be taking part in the fighting services or as a volunteer in one of the branches of civil defense. If so you will report for duty in accordance with the instructions you have received.

You may be engaged in work essential to the prosecution of war for the maintenance of the life of the people – in factories, in transport, in public utility concerns or in the supply of other necessaries of life. If so, it is of vital importance that you should carry on with your jobs.

Now may God bless you all. May He defend the right. It is the evil things that we shall be fighting against – brute force, bad faith, in-

justice, oppression and persecution – and against them I am certain that the right will prevail.

Later that day France, New Zealand, Australia and India joined Britain its declaration of war and a British ship was attacked and sunk by a German submarine. The ship's name seemed ominous for Greece; it was the SS Athenia.

We stayed home that Sunday. I never did find out what happened to the man on the teetering ladder.

Britain's Prime Minister, Winston Churchill.

CHAPTER 7 : *I GO TO JAIL*

Despite my screams in the classroom during the gas mask demonstration, I was anxious to start school. I envied my sisters' ability to read books, magazines and newspapers. My father's large collection of leather-bound books, behind the glass doors of a big carved walnut bookcase, was tantalizing. I was allowed to remove any book I wished. The illustrations alone, like the colored ones in *The Life of Animals*, stimulated my mind aplenty. But I understood that unknown treasures were hidden in the words.

Finally the day came. I was presented with a handsome school bag that could be carried by a handle or on my back, which I preferred as it was soldierly. Carrying it by hand was for girls.

Mama led me to the Second Elementary School, a two-story building with metal windows divided into squares. This school and my life there will feature later when I describe the war's effects, so I must briefly introduce you to it.

A covered playground was bordered by shrubbery and eucalyptus trees. My teacher, Mrs Paleologou, was overweight but beautiful. A mole on her nose was the focus of the class's attention until we got used to it. Some children were dressed as nicely as I; poorer ones wore clothes that were clean but frayed. Some children cried when their mothers had to leave and clung desperately to them. I was bewildered as I saw nothing threatening.

I recall nothing else of my momentous first day except that as I walked home and turned the corner to our house, a smell of fried potatoes reached my nostrils. My mother had prepared my favorite food as a celebratory surprise. Its beloved aroma, which I took for granted at that time, would come back to taunt me during the war. But this wasn't all. Awaiting me on the table was a brand-new black slate. Tied to its wooden frame with a string was a little sponge.

In that first year of my schooling I was ready to conquer the world.

Unfortunately, so was Hitler.

• • •

I was happy in class. Monsieur Champollion, the famous scholar who extracted the secret of Egyptian hieroglyphics from the mysterious Rosetta Stone, couldn't have felt a more triumphant sense of discovery. It turned out that I was precocious and I reveled in this. Other children grappled with our reading book; I raced through it in a couple of weeks. I could draw as well. I seemed brighter than I was because my eavesdropping on my elders' conversations peppered my vocabulary with adult phrases even when I had no idea what they meant. One day our teacher showed us a picture of a cow and asked us to describe its eyes.

"The eyes of the cow are round," said one child.

"The eyes of the cow are brown," said another.

I proclaimed: "The eyes of the cow look vague and are without expression." Mrs Paleologou's eyes became as big and round as the cow's.

A boy in my class, Giannis Velonias, and I became inseparable. We still were more than seven decades later. His grandmother lived next to the school and we visited her for refreshments.

We already had an eye for the girls. During recess Giannis and I played "horses and riders" with two girls. When we were the horses the girls used the straps of our pants as reins, but as they galloped innocently around the yard we'd use their dresses as reins, lifting these as high as possible to see their panties. I fell in love with one of the smartest girls in class, the teacher's pet. I'd previously been smitten with just about all my mother's and sisters' friends, but this time it was true love.

"I'm going to kiss her," I confided to Giannis.

"You're going to get in trouble," he cautioned.

"I don't care. I'll do it."

One afternoon after school I waited by the gate. As my beloved came out I embraced her and planted a juicy kiss on her cheek. She pushed me away and ran home crying. The next day Mama was summoned to the school. She returned home pretending to be angry but was obviously amused. She went through the motions of scolding me, and Mrs Paleologou's manner toward me for the next little while made it clear that if my mother was amused, she was not.

• • •

Our *Er-Ce-Ah* radio went on upsetting the adults, producing ever more intriguing words that were instantly added to my elders' continuingly worried conversations. *Western Front. Maginot Line. Low Countries. Dunkirk.*

For months a major theme in the news was the terrible conflict raging in the skies over Britain: the struggle for aerial supremacy that was to go down in history as the Battle of Britain, a phrase introduced by the new British Prime Minister, Winston Churchill. In June of 1940, speaking to the House of Commons, he warned of the trials to come. *What General Weygand has called the Battle of France is over,* he said. *I expect that the Battle of Britain is about to begin. Upon this battle depends the survival of Christian civilization. Upon it depends our own British life, and the long continuity of our institutions and our Empire. The whole fury and might of the enemy must very soon be turned on us. Hitler knows that he will have to break us in this island or lose the war... Let us therefore brace ourselves to our duties, and so bear ourselves, that if the British Empire and its Commonwealth last for a thousand years, men will still say, "This was their finest hour."*

• • •

From July through October German bombs rained down upon the United Kingdom, with the Luftwaffe and the Royal Air Force locked in a massive, deadly struggle for ownership of Britain's air space.

The dramatic images of heroic air battle percolated deep into my imagination. Planes shooting down other planes was something I could understand. I discussed the news with my friend Boubis. We concluded that the English were good and the Germans bad. In view of this thoughtful finding we decided that we, too, should contribute to the war effort. For this we commandeered a neighborhood almond tree, the only one we could find with low, climbable branches. We each chose a branch and, pretending to be English, declared our branch to be our fighter plane. While communicating in nonsense language (as the movies had shown us that fighter pilots invariably did), we aimed our invisible machine guns toward the sky or the trees around us and fired at butterflies, crawling lady birds, shiny green scarab beetles and grasshoppers, all of which were, unfortunately for them, deemed to be German. They were no longer trophies to be brought home live to be shown to our parents and then set free. We now wanted them dead.

While these aggressive games enabled me to show my fearlessness, the cloud of adult fear over our house grew larger and darker. Mama was stricken with terror. Again and again she repeated, "One of these days we will see the Germans on our doorstep, one of these days we'll see the Germans on our doorstep ..."

She was right and she was wrong. Fate was not to permit Mama to see the Germans on our doorstep.

But the rest of us would.

• • •

In addition to fighting German insects in my first year of school, and gaining a reputation as a womanizer, I became a jailbird.

Mama loved me dearly and forgave my misdeeds, but her love wasn't unconditional. She was a disciplinarian who taught me manners, respect, human values and responsibility. For example, a block from our house, on the square called Perivolaki, Little Orchard, was a kiosk where I spent my pennies on candy. The owner, crippled from some war, was an unsmiling but polite man. In the early nineteen-forties he was succeeded by his daughter Militsa, who gave up her studies to support the family.

At that kiosk Mama had given me my first serious lesson in morality. On a warm summer evening about a year before starting school, I'd walked to the kiosk and spotted an open box of chocolates. I quietly took one without paying and returned home, happily munching. Mama asked me where I'd got the chocolate. I told her. I'd never seen her so angry. Taking my hand, she led me back to the kiosk.

"You see this boy?" she asked the owner. "He's my son. He stole a chocolate from you and I'm ashamed." She paid him and took me home. On the way she gave me a talking-to about acceptable behavior that I never forgot.

But now I sinned again.

One day after school a classmate invited me to go to his house and play on his swing. After a couple of hours I went home to learn that as it hadn't occurred to me to tell anyone where I was, the cry had gone out that I was missing. The neighborhood had been searched with high emotion. On finding no trace of me, my family had alerted the police. Half of the small police force of Kallithea had started combing the area. The worst was feared.

Mama decided I needed another lesson. She took me to the police station and asked the officer in charge to put me in jail. They exchanged glances, as adults do, and he locked me in a cell. They stood looking at me through the bars, expecting tears and cringing remorse.

But this time I was in no mood to be rehabilitated. I sat on the bench and stared back sullenly, thinking how stupid adults could be. After all, I hadn't done anything wrong. I hadn't stolen anything. You don't put people in jail for being late. So I resolved to spoil their game. Pretending to be Cheeta, the chimpanzee in Tarzan movies, I leaped about, scratched myself and made ape noises. The officer shook his head. "You have a very lively child on your hands, Madam." He unlocked the cell and sent my yet-again embarrassed mother and me on our way.

• • •

Mama taught me not just about decency but also about the preciousness of life. She bought silkworm eggs that we incubated together, feeding the hatchlings with mulberry leaves on our table until they spun silk cocoons. It was she who urged me to set my string-leashed scarab beetles free. Her concern to imbue my wayward mind with moral understanding acquired a lasting poignancy when, as a man, I realized the tense and difficult backdrop against which I'd received the gifts of her tenderness. These are illustrated by the irony of August 15, 1940.

In the Greek Orthodox Church that day is the Feast of the Assumption of the Virgin Mary, when every girl with the name Maria, or any of its many variations, celebrates her Name Day. Pilgrims journey to the island of Tinos, my Yaya's birthplace, where an icon of Mary, the mother of Jesus, is kept. The infirm pray there to be cured. Tinos is thus a Greek counterpart of the shrine of Lourdes in France, and

August 15 is a day of faith in life and of hope that a transcendent dignity can somehow lift us beyond our human frailties. On that holy day in 1940, Greece dispatched the navy cruiser Elli to Tinos to honor the occasion. As she lay at anchor in the harbor, the Italian submarine Delfino torpedoed and sank her. Italy hadn't yet declared war on Greece. Nine men died on the Elli. Twenty-four were wounded.

Everyone was incredulous. The talk was suddenly not about Germans but Italians. Newspaper vendors went around shouting the news. It was reported that the Elli had been sunk "by a submarine of unknown nationality", but few doubted that the submarine was Italian.

A neighbor asked my father, who had lived many years in Mussolini's Italy, for his opinion.

"Of course it's the Italians," he said, "but our government is trying to avoid giving them an excuse to start the war. We're trying to stay out of it."

In our neighborhood people stood on the streets, holding a newspaper with its bold headlines and shaking a fist as they cursed the Italians. Men shook their heads somberly. "There will be war soon. It's unavoidable now."

Women crossed themselves. "It's sacrilege. God will punish them for this!"

That September we went to the Etoile open-air cinema, days before it closed for winter. There we received the latest news of the air battles raging over Britain. Again and again the Germans were hurled back until, by late October, Hitler and his generals were accepting that they weren't going to destroy Britain's air defense capability. At least not yet. Although Germany would continue its air raids on Britain, the air conflict of 1940 wound down in Britain's favor.

The vision of a tiny, unprepared Britain repelling Hitler's aerial horde had a magnificent effect on our morale. When the news bulletin at the Etoile that September told the audience that three British planes had perished, I asked Litsa what "perished" meant. She didn't know either but to be smart she said it meant, "They won."

We applauded enthusiastically.

The Duce, Benito Mussolini.

CHAPTER 8 : *ON THE BACKS OF MULES*

My eyes opened with a start. From either side of the big baroque bed I shared with my mother, the little relief brass cherubs looked down at me benignly, as always.

But in contrast to their familiar smiles, a blood-curdling wail assailed my ears.

I glanced about. Mama was gone. I was alone.

The ear-splitting sound tearing through our open windows was the scream of the Town Hall air raid siren that I called The Chinaman. But this wasn't another drill. This time the shattering noise wouldn't stop.

It went on and on and on, relentlessly.

I got out of bed. Hoisting myself up with my elbows on the cold terrazzo windowsill, my feet dangling, I peered out at a gray day. My friend the eucalyptus tree swayed back and forth in the morning breeze, mirroring the agitation of the people milling about our street. Neighbors, Mama and my sisters were all outside, talking animatedly.

It was cool at that early hour but the mild chill was not the cause of the sudden shiver sweeping through me. The piercing, sinister, incessant din of The Chinaman smothered everything. My teeth began rattling. Trembling uncontrollably, I slid to the floor, dressed and went out.

My mother was pale. I leaned my head against her in the street like a kitten seeking reassurance. Nestled in her arm, I stood listening to a chaos of voices.

{ 63 }

It was October 28, 1940.

Italy was at war with Greece.

• • •

A few hours earlier, around three a.m., Italy's ambassador had awoken the head of the Greek government, Ioannis Metaxas, with a note demanding Greece's agreement to a military occupation of its territory by Italy. The alternative was war. A compliant response was required by six a.m.

Metaxas immediately rejected the demand, telling the ambassador in French, the language of diplomacy: *"Alors, c'est la guerre."* ("So then, we're at war.") At five thirty Italy invaded Greece via Albania.

For almost a year Italy had waged an undeclared war of nerves against Greece. Italian radio broadcasts constantly vilified Greece, claiming that Greeks were responsible for incidents that insulted Italy. Then the Elli had been sunk. To avoid giving the Italians any excuse for aggression, Greece's government had gone out of its way to avoid blaming Italy for the sinking, even though Greeks knew very well what was happening. But Greece had also made it clear that it wouldn't sit still if invaded.

Benito Mussolini, Italy's fascist dictator, paid no heed.

Mussolini had visions of a new Roman Empire with himself as emperor. He envied Hitler's steps to build a new German Reich at the expense of Czechoslovakia, Poland, Denmark, Norway, Holland, Belgium and France, and he wasn't happy that Germany's actions were relegating Italy to a minor role in world affairs.

For a time Mussolini had thought that if he waited until victory for Hitler was assured, he could enter the war as a latecomer and share the spoils with Germany. But Hitler's plans didn't fit well with these ambitions. For instance, Mussolini coveted France's overseas possessions; Hitler wanted to leave them undisturbed. The Führer didn't want to goad the French fleet into defecting to the British. Also, he wanted Germany to seem kind to a vanquished foe in the eyes of the world.

Similarly, Hitler preferred to leave Yugoslavia and Greece alone for the time being, avoiding anything that would provoke Britain to help them, since this would give the British a foothold in the region. He wished to focus instead on the Soviet Union. He had it in mind to get around to Yugoslavia and Greece later, at which time he expected to be in a position to achieve his ends by political pressure and intimidation rather than having to invest valuable military resources.

But Mussolini didn't want to wait. He craved immediate glory. In 1936 he'd seized the African country of Ethiopia, and in 1939, Albania. Now his eyes fell impatiently on Greece, a poor country which had suffered through several wars since the beginning of the century. Greece had no arms industry to speak of. Its forces were ill-equipped, mostly with obsolete weapons, including planes from World War One. Spare parts for its military were unavailable since all came from countries which Germany now controlled.

Mussolini's sycophants encouraged him to believe the Greeks would be a pushover. So, without consulting Hitler, he decided to take Greece on.

• • •

Overnight Kallithea became a sea of blue and white. Spontaneously, with no official prompting, Greek flags that had been in storage, and taken out only on special occasions, appeared on balconies and improvised flagpoles.

Patriotic marches issued from our *Er-Ce-Ah* all day. Patriotic poems were recited. Broadcasters were careful not to raise the people's hopes. After all, the adults were saying, Italy had over 40 million people; we had some seven million. They had many ships and planes; we had few. Some said only a miracle could save the country.

But it seemed miracles just might be attainable. Without waiting for their draft notifications, Greek men of military age and beyond, from all walks of life, rushed to recruitment centers. They came from cities, towns, from remote villages and islands, on every public conveyance. They came from the islands on steamers and sailboats; on land by train, on horses, on the backs of mules, on foot. Within weeks they were heading for the front.

The fresh-faced young men of our neighborhood turned out in ill-fitting uniforms, bidding farewell to family and friends with brave smiles and embraces as everyone tearfully wished them good luck and victory. At Kallithea's tram depot men clustered on the steps of the old trams bound for recruitment centers in Athens. People gathered at the plateia to wave at the recruits and shout, "Give them a good lesson!" or "Avenge Elli and the sacrilege of Tinos!" The rousing reply, "We'll throw them in the sea!", became a rallying cry that lasted throughout the war.

There was no time for boot camp training. After being issued with creased uniforms at the recruiting centers, the men boarded flimsy cattle trains headed north. At every stop at towns or villages, throngs waited with bread, food, water and cakes to refresh the soldiers. Since there were no train lines to the mountains, all private cars except taxis were requisitioned to carry troops and equipment as far north as the roads allowed. From there it was a matter of walking, with supplies borne by mules and human shoulders. Women from the towns and villages of the Epirus region volunteered to carry burdens to the front lines.

Even my friend Boubi's crippled Uncle Dimitrakis, born with several handicaps, was drafted. He was assigned to care for the mules destined for the front. One day he showed up in an unkempt uniform, dragging his useless leg, his paralyzed arm tucked in his shirt. He told Boubi and me grandly that despite his lowly station he'd been shown how to use grenade launchers. I couldn't understood much of what he said because he had a speech impediment and dribbled from the side of his mouth. But his eyes flashed with the resolve to stand up to Mussolini.

• • •

My father was recalled to active service.

Demobilized in 1921 with the rank of lieutenant, he'd been retained in the reserves. Now he was re-commissioned as a first lieutenant. Like many other former soldiers of his age, he had to go to a tailor to have a couple of uniforms made. His generation's old uniforms, hung as mementoes in their closets for almost two decades, would no longer fit. He also went to a cobbler for a pair of boots. These were immaculately crafted. When my father brought them home and examined them, he saw that the cobbler had beautifully inscribed on the bottom of one, *Kalo Dyrrachion!*, which translates idiomatically into "Happy Dyrrachion!" Dyrrachion, or Durrës, was the town in Albania from which the Italians had launched their attack on Greece. The cobbler's inscription was an encouragement to my father and his fellow soldiers to kick the Italians back to Dyrrachion and beyond.

Others in my family followed my father into the military. My Uncle Alfredos, who was a judge, was drafted as a private, as was cousin Vagelis Loizos from the island of Chios. Vagelis drove supply and ammunition trucks.

The first time my father's portly, uniformed figure stepped out of our house, the neighbors applauded and wished him well. At first my mother and sisters were in tears because they feared he'd be sent to the front. But because he'd lived in Italy for years as a successful businessman, his Italian was excellent, so he was assigned to the Prisoner of War Selection Center in Athens. This was an important position. My father was in charge of processing Italian prisoners: registering them, recording their names and ranks, notifying the Red Cross of their existence and transferring them to internment camps in Egypt or elsewhere. He took a tram into Athens very early every morning and returned very late.

My father's workplace was known to us simply as The Barracks. In the nineteenth century it had housed a training center for non-commissioned officers, and later a military hospital which, designed in the light of Louis Pasteur's discoveries about microbes, consisted not of a single large building but several separate ones, so as to obstruct the transmission of infection between wards. Now those buildings housed my father, his military staff and the prisoners who were temporarily in his charge.

It was not just a physical place but a world that reflected all the pain and the strangeness of war. I would get to know it well, and the faces that I would see there were to stay in my mind for decades.

• • •

The time of the blackout began.

Everyone bought rolls of paper, tape, glue and thumbtacks. Men, women and children fastened the double-thickness black paper to wooden shutters. Tape was glued in rectangular and diagonal patterns over every windowpane to keep glass from shattering when bombs fell. The streetlights went out. Lights on streetcars, buses and private vehicles were painted blue except for a small horizontal slit that, as far as I could see, served no purpose whatsoever. Total darkness descended on Kallithea.

Everyone spoke fearfully of air raid shelters and the bombing of civilians that had taken place in the Spanish town of Guernica and the Dutch city of Rotterdam. Most Kallithea houses were old, lacking the basements and reinforced concrete floors of newer homes. My resourceful mother secured permission from a contractor, Mr Karagiannis, to use one of his unfinished buildings, a block away from us, as a shelter for our family. This coup came none too soon. Almost immediately The Chinaman began screeching his air raid warnings and we were scrambling for refuge.

But so powerful is the human ability to adapt, and to grow accustomed to almost anything, that soon these periodic flights for our survival became routine.

When The Chinaman screamed at night, my half-asleep father gathered me up and carried me on his shoulders through the lightless streets to our shelter. From this bouncing perch I asked him through the din, in jerky, hiccup-like phrases, "Why are they doing this to us, Baba?"

He replied breathlessly, without breaking his run, "Don't ask me now, son. It's hard to explain."

CHAPTER 9 : *THE CLICKING OF THE BEADS*

Our *Er-Ce-Ah* radio's news from the front was initially vague. Then it became encouraging.

We heard how, in the Epirus region bordering Albania, General Charalambos Katsimitros disobeyed orders from the General Staff to retreat to a safer strategic position. He and his men stayed put at a place called Kalpaki, refusing to budge. The men were locals, defending their homes. Armed with this fierce motivation they stopped an overwhelmingly superior Italian force, forcing it into a defensive position.

We heard how, in the Pindus Mountains, Colonel Konstantinos Davakis, our neighbor from Kallithea, led some two thousand men in successfully blocking the advance of over nine thousand Italian soldiers. They held the enemy off from late October until Greek reinforcements reached them a couple of weeks later. Colonel Davakis took a bullet in his chest but survived.

That the poorly-equipped Greeks held their positions at all was amazing enough. That they gave the superior numbers of their better-armed enemy such a fight was even more remarkable. Most astonishing of all was that only a week before, many if not all of the Greek combatants had been civilians. Moreover, after walking to the front through miles of mud, with local women accompanying them to help carry their supplies through areas without trains or roads, these soldiers fought in severe conditions, with snowstorms and flooded rivers, at elevations of five to six thousand feet. Yet in a week they trapped and defeated Mussolini's elite Julia Mountain Division, capturing some five thousand Italians and their equipment, and destroying the central thrust of the Italians' three-phase invasion plan.

"Virgin Mary punished them for Tinos," said some. A story went around that soldiers had seen the Holy Mother's image hovering over the mountains of Pindus.

Church bells pealed throughout Greater Athens. A few days later, long lines of captured Italians in olive-green uniforms were marched through Athens to my father's transfer station, The Barracks. The prisoners' feathered Alpine hats prompted people to call these men *oi kokorofteroi* ("rooster feathers"), which was to be a derisive Greek name for Italian soldiers for the rest of the war.

• • •

The Italians bombed the port of Piraeus, near Athens, and other Greek towns. They weren't very successful in hitting military targets but they did kill civilians. This created widespread dread that at any moment death might rain down on us. Even though no planes came near Athens, the sirens wailed every day.

Because our original air raid shelter was small and cramped, my energetic mother found another: the basement of a family friend, Dr Kapalas, whose two-story house was almost diagonally across from our old shelter. The concrete ceiling was reinforced with heavy wooden beams anchored to the floor. It seemed capable of withstanding a direct bomb hit without burying us alive. Into this space our family crowded during many air raids alongside the Kapalas family and the Symeonidis family, who lived on the second floor: old Mr Symeonidis, a taciturn, erect, white-haired patriarch, his two sons, Nikos and Euthimis, and his daughter Nitsa. During the raids the elder Symeonidis sat silently in a corner playing with his kombolói, his worry beads. Before the bombs fell there were often long and tense periods of suspenseful, absolute silence broken only by the constant click-click of the beads, which drove my mother out of her mind.

"When can we go home, mama?" I would ask.

"When the siren sounds the all clear."

"When's that?"

"We don't know."

And we'd all sit there for a long time, no one saying a word. Against the background of the deep and pregnant hush, the incessant clicking of Mr Simeonidis' beads as they hit one another, again and again and again, became loud drumbeats that steadily and relentlessly wore down my poor mother's nerves. The old gentleman sat impassively staring at the bare cement floor while his fingers worked the beads, and it was as if he were using them to count the seconds that fate had left to us before a bomb descended.

• • •

November of 1940 brought more good news. The Greek army was counter-attacking the Italians on every front.

One day the church bells rang out and kept ringing continuously. Since there was no longer any sound of private road traffic, the bells held dominion over the rooftops and their music reverberated throughout the entire Plain of Attica. Big bells and small bells alike chimed in. People spilled into the streets to investigate and were told that our soldiers had taken the Albanian town of Koritsá, a key strategic possession, crushing the Italian force there even though the Greeks had no tanks and virtually no anti-tank weapons. Our men had captured equipment and prisoners.

There was dancing and embracing in the streets. Newly derisive cartoons of Mussolini and his soldiers filled the newspapers. Popular Greek and Italian songs were parodied in ditties ridiculing the Italians. And this wasn't the only music that this era produced. In addition to the satirical tunes that poked fun at the enemy, our *Er-Ce-Ah* began to bring us moving new songs imbued with a wartime sense of Greek togetherness that would last long after the war. The British had Vera Lynn (*We'll Meet Again*), the Germans Lale Andersen (*Lili Marlene*). Greeks had Sofia Vembo, whose remarkable voice was equally suited to mocking our foes and stirring the hearts of Greeks with hope. Her lyrics were on everyone's lips. My grandmother frequently prodded me to sing them too. I needed little prodding.

When the Germans later occupied Greece, Sofia Vembo was one of the first people their Italian allies wanted to see locked up. But by she eluded them by fleeing to Egypt from where her songs continued to torment the Axis and inspire us. To this day I can still remember the tunes and almost all their lyrics. The lively, charming pre-war Italian song *Campagnola Bella* was changed to *Koroido Mussolini* ("Sucker Mussolini"), the Spanish song *Perlita* became *Benito*, the Greek song *Mari* was adapted to *Soddu*, the name of an inept Italian general replaced by Mussolini, and so on.

Sofia Vembo had no tanks or guns, but she wounded our enemy magnificently.

• • •

On December 1 all the bells of Greater Athens pealed once more, this time to celebrate our army's capture of the Italian-held Albanian town of Pogradec.

A few days later another orchestration marked the pushing of the Italians back toward the Adriatic Sea. And this time I had my own reason for gladness. I turned seven.

Italian radio was calling Greek soldiers barbarians because they used bayonets, to which our men had to resort to spare precious ammunition. Some Italian prisoners at The Barracks had confessed that Greek bayonet charges terrified them.

My father had heard by this time that our soldiers were fighting mostly with captured Italian weapons. Britain's military in Egypt had thus begun shipping us ammunition captured from the Italian army in North Africa.

I seldom saw my father now. He left when I was asleep and he returned home very late. In my few memories of him from those days it is his weary voice that comes back to me, discussing the war in the brief intervals between his duties.

We greeted Saint Nicholas Day, December 6, my father's name day, without guests that year.

And without my father.

• • •

While men battled one another on the earth and in the skies with such fury and tools as they could muster, human power for good and evil alike was dwarfed by the awesome presence of the winter that ended 1940. The elements visited their majestic force impartially on both Greek and Italian. In the mountains snow rose meters high. Our *Er-Ce-Ah* and the newspapers reported the Italian state radio as stating that Italy's reversals at the front were due to inclement weather, as if our soldiers were not facing the same conditions.

Our freezing troops lacked such basic items as gloves, socks and scarves. A program called *I Fanella tou Stratiotou* ("The Soldier's Vest") began. Female Greeks, from grandmothers to girls of seven, got to work knitting warm clothing for the men in combat. The completed items were taken to collection centers from where they were sent to the front line. My sisters tirelessly knitted balaclavas (ski masks), pullovers, gloves and socks. My mother, who was always involved in civic affairs, took the initiative in Kallithea to gather these gifts and expedite their delivery. Princess Frederika sent her a letter of appreciation.

This mass outpouring of tenderness from the kitchens and living rooms of Greece meant much to both the grateful soldiers and their benefactors. It brought into the pit of war not only the bodily warmth provided by the physical garments but, no less valuably, the psychological warmth and human solidarity that came from kindness toward soldiers who were at one and the same time strangers and countrymen. To those at home it brought a feeling of contact with distant, faceless men, many no more than boys, who were fighting for our security. The fleeting nature of this contact made it wrench the heart all the more. The newspapers published names of soldiers who wanted to correspond with girls at home in their rare moments of rest. My sister Alexandra put her name and address inside the many pairs of socks she knitted. She received letters from two young men somewhere on the front. One I recall only as Sotiris. The other was Vassos Ploumbidis, an educated, articulate young man. He and my sister wrote to each other until the collapse of the Albanian front when Germany invaded Greece.

Then the letters stopped.

Business boomed for Mr Spyropoulos' haberdashery in Kallithea, which sold yarn for the knitting campaign. Sometimes he couldn't meet demand.

But his sales of black dye doubled as well.

Alexandra at The Barracks, flanked by her father and her brother in his Evzone costume.

CHAPTER 10 : *THE LOST MEN*

A new chain of events now began, not caused by the war yet inextricably associated with wartime images that would vividly define that time for me forever.

Mama was diagnosed with cancer. She had surgery at Evangelismos Hospital, a ten-minute walk from my father's workplace. For two weeks or so my sisters and I went into Athens daily to be with Mama. I returned home with my sisters, or in late evening with my father.

It was the first of several circumstances that were to give me special glimpses of the effects of war. Few places provide these more graphically than a hospital.

Previously I'd wandered briefly into Greece's politics outfitted in a fascist uniform. Now, on my excursions to the hospital, my sisters always made me wear our national costume, the Evzone outfit named for Greece's mountain troops. They dressed me thus not to rub salt into the wounds of Italian prisoners at the hospital but to boost the morale of our own soldiers being treated there. To the wounded men who packed the wards, a little boy in national dress could not but draw smiles.

"What do you want to be when you grow up?" they asked. I answered: "An aviator."

"Do you have a girlfriend?" they asked. I blushed.

I roamed the corridors at will; my innocuous looks and patriotic garb were my passport. I witnessed things no child should see: stretchers with men crying in agony and calling for their mothers, or suffering in silence. On a rare occasions when I was turned back from my explorations, I saw a sheet-covered person on a stretcher and asked a nurse, "Is he dead?"

"You shouldn't be here. Where are your parents? Go back to them."

I saw a cart piled with bloody bandages being wheeled along the corridor.

"Where do you throw them away?" I asked the man.

"We don't throw them away. We take them to the autoclave."

"What's an autoclave?"

"It's a machine where we clean the bandages to use them again because we don't have any more."

I passed the open door of a private room where a man in pajamas sat on the edge of his bed. He was handsome, with thick gray hair. He beckoned; I entered. He put me on his lap, kissed my cheek and stroked my head.

"What's your name?"

"Vagelis."

"And your big name?" (Surname.)

"Loizos."

"Come on, my brave boy," he murmured, "grow up and give us a hand to save our country."

Tears welled in his eyes. He put me down gently with a pat. Bored, I turned to leave. A couple of nurses who'd watched the scene told me reverently, "This is Colonel Davakis!"

With a fleeting glance at the man, who still gazed at me intently with moist eyes, I left. Only later would I realize that I'd sat on the lap of the hero of Pindus, for whose extraordinary victory against the Italians the bells of Athens had pealed. This son of Kallithea was also a decorated hero of World War One, in which his lungs were permanently damaged in a gas attack. He'd come out of semi-retirement to help defend his country anew. Shot through the chest by an Italian sniper at Pindus, he told an officer who came to his aid, "Let me be, count me as dead. See that they don't take your positions. Get going!"

But he'd been brought to Athens along with some five thousand Italian prisoners who were now in The Barracks, being processed by my father.

• • •

Davakis wasn't the only hero I encountered in the hospital. One day I saw a great commotion. A large group of nurses, doctors and civilians surrounded a naval officer and his entourage. I attached myself to this officer as he toured the wards to rousing salutations. Hearing everyone respectfully repeating the name Papanikolis, I rushed back to Mama and told her excitedly that I'd seen Mr Papanikolis. She laughed and explained that Mr Papanikolis had been dead almost a century. He was a naval hero of Greece's War of Independence against the Turks in 1821. A Greek submarine had been named after him and the officer I'd seen was its daring captain, Miltiadis Iatridis. The Papanikolis, of 1920s vintage, was so antiquated and ramshackle that foreign military attaches called it a coffin, but under Iatridis' command it created havoc among enemy ships ferrying troops and supplies between Italy and Albania. Mama related the incident to all visitors, to their amusement and my embarrassment.

• • •

In addition to my solitary expeditions I accompanied my sisters on their ward rounds to visit soldiers, who enthralled us with tales of their experiences. Mortar fire and shrapnel wounds were common, and many had lost limbs to frostbite. Thanasis, a young man from a northern village in Epirus, described his Hotchkiss machine gun with great affection, pronouncing it Hotsikesh, and told us what he had done with it to the "rooster feathers".

"I sure took care of them with my Hotsikesh. They almost never reached our lines. When they did, we put the bayonets on our rifles and rushed them."

A few days later Alexandra and I walked from the hospital along Vasilissis Sofias Avenue and saw a long line of forlorn Italians, hundreds of them, being marched from the train station, a mile or so away, to The Barracks. Their clothes, though cleaned and deloused, still bore the traces of the struggle in the mountains. They dragged their feet in weary resignation. Like all the soldiers I saw at the hospital and The Barracks, both Greek and Italian, they were lost men, men who should have been at home with their families and ordinary occupations. A handful of armed Greek guards accompanied them. People lining the street gawked silently. Alexandra and I, too, stopped and watched. Beside us was a vendor of koulourakia, the circular little breads with sesame seeds that are ubiquitous in Athens. Alexandra bought me one. Suddenly a Greek walked up to the prisoners with an open pack of cigarettes. Hands reached out for them gratefully. Then the vendor next to us offered the prisoners his tray of koulourakia.

A guard warned him, "They don't have any money."

"It doesn't matter," replied the vendor. "They have mothers too."

The tray was soon empty.

• • •

I was now seeing more of my father. I became a fixture at The Barracks: everybody knew I was the First Lieutenant's son and, as in the hospital, I gallivanted without restriction. Not only did my national costume seem not to offend any prisoner, but many cosseted me.

The headquarters of The Barracks was a stone building. My father worked in a large second-floor room crowded with desks and tables where uniformed staff worked non-stop. Maps and notices covered the walls. Messengers scurried constantly. My father's desk, at the front window, was flanked on either side by two long tables. A dozen captured Italian officers sat here, their green uniforms clean and ironed as if ready for inspection. My father had selected some of the best-educated, high-ranking Italians to help him process the endless stream of their countrymen pouring in.

New arrivals entered in small groups and lined up at the long tables. The officers recorded their names to notify their families, giving each prisoner sixty drachmas spending money provided by the Red Cross. Like me, some prisoners were privileged to have a free run of the place. These trusties served Italian and Greek officers alike, bringing them coffee and running errands. The Italian officers seemed amiable, ordinary men and were courteously and decently treated, especially by my father. To all appearances they and their Greek custodians might have been colleagues rather than deadly enemies.

There were times when this overriding humanity could not but inject laughter into even so serious a situation. Once my attractive sister Maria, aged nineteen, sat at my father's desk awaiting his return. The Italian officers, not realizing she spoke Italian fluently, discussed her in the language of young men who hadn't seen a woman for months. She sat unperturbed, pretending ignorance. Some Greek officers came in to talk to the Italians and asked for my father so he could interpret. Maria told them she didn't know where he was but that she could interpret. She launched into excellent Italian, to the Italian officers' mortification. After the Greek officers left, they embarrassedly apologized, begging Maria not to say anything to my father. She never mentioned the incident to him, but the story made Mama laugh so hard her stitches hurt.

• • •

I often went into the prisoners' quarters. The Greek sentry always let me through but kept an eye on me. Most prisoners were friendly and played with me, chattering away in Italian, of which I understood not a word. The few who weren't very friendly wore black shirts and were hard-core fascists. An exception among these was Mario. Our soldiers had taught him to sing the mocking song *Koroido Mussolini* ("Sucker Mussolini"), which he'd happily sing for a cigarette.

"A real soldier": Evangelos with Mannlicher rifle.

Once, the sentry decided it would be especially amusing for Mario to sing this song at the request of a child. Letting me pass into the prisoners' quarters, he told me, "Go and ask him to sing "Sucker Mussolini" for you." I made my request and Mario duly sang it for me with brio, ridiculing the Duce.

• • •

My Father had this Luger ...

One day an itinerant photographer arrived with an ancient wooden camera on a tripod. Greek soldiers of all ranks got him to take souvenir pictures. A sentry suggested a photo of me holding his Mannlicher rifle.

"It will make him look like a real soldier," he told Alexandra. He made sure it was safe and handed it to me. It was so heavy I could hardly lift it. It took great effort for me to hold it and pose long enough for the photographer to take the picture. But after a few minutes of waiting, the photo was developed and everyone thought it was marvelous. The strain of holding up the rifle had given me an expression of great resolve, as if I were about to rid our land of all invaders.

• • •

On December 8 the church bells rang a long, long time. The Greek army had taken the towns of Argyrokastro and Delvinaki. We seemed unstoppable. New prisoners wore different uniforms and insignia, representing the variety of divisions Mussolini was desperately hurling at us. But there were also more mutilated, gaunt Greek soldiers in the hospital.

When I stayed late at The Barracks my father and I walked together past the hospital on our way to Omonoia railroad station. He carried a flashlight to find his way in the blackout, and he would say goodnight to Mama by flashing the light briefly on the window of her room as we passed. We'd then take the tram to Kallithea, where'd we'd make our way home through the pitch-black streets.

• • •

I was in Mama's hospital room when the doctor removed the metal clips from the long incision on her stomach. My father brought her home in a taxi. He supported her to the threshold and asked her to wait. He came in, got a long metal ruler from his desk, laid it down and asked my mother to step on it.

"Siderenia," he said as she entered. ("Of iron may you be.") Despite having lived abroad all these years and being a man of the world, my father had retained some of the folklore of the island folk.

Mama recuperated in bed for a week or two while visitors kept her company. And then she was up, and back at work again as the binding presence of our home.

Within her was an iron for which no folklore was needed.

Two airmen with Maria and Evangelos

CHAPTER 11 : *CREEPING SPIDER*

With my mother back home it was my turn to be "demobilized": when I joined my sisters on visits to The Barracks now, it was without my patriotic costume.

Mama plunged back into her philanthropic activities with renewed energy but on a more limited scale. Her top priority was to resume management of our household. Although we'd survived while she was in the hospital she returned to us in the spirit of a general who, inspecting his troops after an absence from them, felt that only the gracious mercy of Providence had saved them from death while they were deprived of his essential leadership. We must have looked starved because Mama immediately bought immense quantities of food. Pasta, beans, chickpeas, lentils, dried figs and raisins suddenly filled the big trunk-like wooden sofa in the dining room to the brim. This may have helped my mother to reconnect with us on more than one level because this container-sofa was much more to her than just a storage device. My father had built it. I was born on it.

Mama secured another air raid shelter for us. She went to Mr Matsis, our family friend whose great stomach had wobbled so entertainingly as he danced the Lambeth Walk at our party in 1938. He lived three blocks away and Mama persuaded him to share his shelter with us. It was in his garden. Most of it was sunk in the ground and was reinforced concrete with thick walls and a bomb-proof roof. It was big enough for a lot of people. Now every time The Chinaman started screaming, we headed there.

• • •

Forces of the British Commonwealth came to Athens, including Royal Air Force squadrons sent to help Greece deal with Italy's overwhelming air superiority. Athenians showered them with invitations to their homes. My mother and sisters invited some to our house. I remember two, Steve and Jim. Noticing that I was obsessed with aviation, Jim drew Hurricane fighter planes and Blenheim bombers for me and taught me a few English words. I recall only one: "blackout". A local photographer, Mr Thodoris, took pictures of us together.

One sunlit morning I heard a plane flying very low over our house. Until that moment I'd known planes only from movies, magazines and books. Seeing and hearing a real airplane for the first time in my life made my heart flutter. I climbed to the terrace and there it was! A biplane of the Greek Air Force.

As it made low passes over the rooftops the pilot waved and we returned his greeting. We knew him! It was Karderinis, a young man who lived a block from us on Lykourgou and Sivitanidou Streets. Everyone shouted, "Go with God! Virgin Mary will protect you!", and, "Come back to us victorious!" He made two more passes and flew away.

"It is a Potez, a P24," said Mrs Metaxas' son, an engineer. "We bought these planes from Poland in exchange for Greek tobacco." He shook his head sadly. "I hope he makes it back. Those planes don't stand a chance against an Italian Fiat or a German Messerschmitt."

I asked him why but his explanation made no sense to me. How could their planes be better than ours? After all, ours had two wings and theirs had only one.

I didn't understand that biplanes were relics of an earlier era. I just knew that they looked good to me.

• • •

There was now no first-hand news from the front. Soldiers didn't come home on leave. Even the dead didn't come home; they were buried at the front. Seriously wounded men went to hospitals where they tended to see only their families. Years later, soldiers would tell me of their lives during this period. One, Marinos George, of the Greek city of Tripoli, was drafted into the army in 1937 and was discharged in 1939 but just a few months later he was recalled to be a cook in an artillery unit.

In Albania, he told me, everything used for cooking was carried on mules. "When we stopped we had to gather the rocks to build the base and gather the wood. Most of the time the wood was wet and it took a lot of time to get the fire going."

The troops' staples were pasta, beans and bread. Ironically, the men often went hungry because of their victories. Marinos would spend hours cooking a meal only to be suddenly ordered to dump it because the unit was advancing. The soldiers had to make do on the move with bread, raisins and Metaxa brandy.

Marinos served under Major Dimitris Kostakis, who walked with a cane and was a master of accurate artillery fire. One of his feats became famous. They spotted an Italian unit across the mountain cooking a meal. Major Kostakis calculated their position so precisely that he was able to deposit a shell right into the cauldron of the unfortunate Italians.

The major was very religious and ordered his men not to curse. To be deprived of the ability to vent their frustrations by cursing was a trying challenge for soldiers on a battlefield. Once some of the men were slaughtering chickens for the pot when one of the birds broke loose and landed in the cauldron of soup that Marinos was cooking. Understandably and by force of habit, he cursed.

Major Kostakis bristled. "Soldier! Don't you know that I do not allow cursing here?"

"Yes sir, Mr Major," Marinos said, coming to fearful attention.

"Do you know that I punish those who violate my orders?"

"Yes sir, Mr Major," Marinos said, fearing the worst.

"Good! Stand at attention and say the Pater Noster."

Marinos tremblingly recited the Lord's Prayer, like a schoolboy being punished for some playground offence.

When he finished, the major told him, "Now get going and finish the food because my boys are hungry. We have a war on our hands and the survival of our country is at stake."

And he hobbled away on his cane.

• • •

Our church bells jubilantly announced more setbacks for Mussolini's troops. The Italians were fighting hard but were being pushed back constantly. Surely, everyone felt, we really would soon throw them into the sea and bring our boys back. But the cost of these victories was becoming more and more apparent. There were shortages of food and other things. The winter of 1940-1941 was bitter. Word was that our soldiers in the Albanian mountains were somehow holding their lines without supplies. My father said our frozen men were subsisting on bread, raisins and cognac. Many had worn out their boots and bound rags on their feet. Frostbite took its toll.

In Albania our forces reached the formidable Klisura Pass, under Italy's control and thought to be impregnable. Italian General Ubaldo Soddu decided to destroy the Greek army there once and for all, brought in additional divisions, and announced that Klisura would be the tomb of the Greek army. However, the Greeks stood their ground, counter-attacked, and took Klisura. The bells of Athens rang again, long and loud.

But a cloud was gathering on the horizon: the prospect of Germany's entry into the onslaught against Greece.

• • •

Around the end of January I was playing on the street in front of our house when a policeman came by telling everyone to put their flags at half-mast because the head of Greece's government, Ioannis Metaxas, had died. The implications of his death for the war effort caused apprehension. Even his political foes worried about what would become of us without a leader. Metaxas had been ill but there were rumors of assassination by foreign agents.

Nonetheless, the country held together and continued to fight.

In March Mussolini launched his biggest assault on us: Operation Primavera (Spring). A massive force, including greatly superior artillery and many men fresh from Italy, were hurled with renewed ferocity against vastly outnumbered Greeks who were exhausted and short of everything, including food and clothing. Italy's large and modern air force bombed and strafed our soldiers relentlessly. The Greeks had a handful of obsolescent planes which they nevertheless put to effective use, loading them with empty tin cans and releasing these over the Italians to send them scurrying for cover. For some ten days the Italians pounded the Greeks but got nowhere. Our men fought day in and day out and repulsed every attempt to break through their lines, until the Italians gave up.

The latest joke in Athens was that Radio Rome stated: "There is nothing new to report on the Greek Front."

• • •

I hardly saw my father now. He spent long hours at The Barracks, where we occasionally visited him and sometimes shared a meal. Greeks of all ranks and all the Italian prisoners had the same food at The Barracks: almost always spinach or cabbage and rice, beans and pasta or beans, bread and fruit. Never meat, which was unaffordable.

On one of our visits I saw a lot of new prisoners being processed. Some wore blue uniforms, some civilian clothes, some Greek uniforms. I was told they were Italian sailors rescued from the sea by British and Greek ships after the Battle of Cape Matapan, where British ships had devastated the Italian fleet. I sat on a chair near my father's desk as he spoke for some time with an Italian in a naval officer's uniform.

"He's the captain of the cruiser Fiume," my father told me later. "His name is Ferruccio Cableri." He shook his head sadly. "Poor man! I wouldn't like to be in his shoes."

March 25, 1941, Greek Independence Day, was a triple celebration, being also both my Name Day and my sister Litsa's. For a reason I can't recall, Mr Archimandritis, the police chief, who was a friend of our family's, sent his limousine to our house and we all piled in for a trip into Athens. I sat in the front seat between Mr Archimandritis and his chauffeur. The city was festooned with flags hanging from every balcony on the main streets: Greek flags, British flags, Chinese flags, and a strange one that looked like a creeping spider.

"We are trying very hard to be everybody's friend," said Mr Archimandritis. "But we are not succeeding."

The spider flag was red with a white circle in the center. In the circle was a black, twisted cross.

I had met the swastika.

CHAPTER 12 : *ENDLESS NIGHT*

On April 6, 1941, a beautiful, sunny day, our *Er-Ce-Ah* radio was filling our house with music when it suddenly went mute.

We all knew what that meant: it was standard procedure for the radio to fall silent when enemy planes appeared on the horizon, so the pilots wouldn't be able to use the radio waves as beacons for their targets. We dropped everything, my mother grabbed me, and we all ran for Mr Matsis' air raid shelter. By the time The Chinaman started his dirge we were almost there. After an hour or so the "all clear" sounded and we returned home, not knowing what the fuss had been about since we hadn't heard any planes.

We soon found out. Germany had declared war on us.

Again our street filled with people. Many, because it was Sunday. They gathered in small gloomy groups speculating on what might happen next. It looked grim, given Hitler's invasions of Poland, Norway, the Low Countries and France. Optimistic sidewalk generals predicted that our heroic soldiers would prevail as they had against the Italians. "After all, we now have the English on our side." Others shook their heads. "We don't stand a chance against them."

The rest of the day passed quietly. There was no news, only rumors. The tension was agonizing. The calm caused it to subside for a spell, but it returned with a vengeance. The air was thick with expectation and foreboding.

Around ten p.m. the silence was broken by The Chinaman's undulating wail. Hearts hammering, everyone ran again for the shelter. This time the warning was justified. The night was filled with the droning of planes, deafening bomb explosions and the rattle of anti-aircraft fire. We cowered in near-darkness: the almost-underground shelter had no electricity. Except for scant, dim light filtering through tiny windows at the top, we relied on a candle which died every time a big blast shook the shelter. Someone would relight it with fumbling fingers but soon it was extinguished by another concussion. Eventually my eyes adjusted. I vaguely made out the shapes of the people crowded around me.

It got worse. Thundering detonations shook the shelter door, reverberating off the cement walls, making our chests and entrails shudder in tune with them.

Women moaned. Children cried. To the rumble from outside was added a babel of sobs, deep sighs, lamentations and prayers to God, Christ and the Virgin Mary. In that diluted half-light, dozens of arms pumped up and down as people crossed themselves, like the connecting rods of some infernal machine whose fuel was pure terror.

I crouched stupefied on the floor in a corner beside Mama, my hands cupping my ears. When the flickering candle went out I kept looking desperately in its direction for it to reappear. Mrs Anna, who lived a few doors down, clasped her only son tightly and shook her fist heavenward, yelling: "Accursed Germans! Accursed Germans! Cursed be the mother that gave you life! How'd you like it if someone else was doing this to your children?"

It seemed the ordeal would never end, but slowly the explosions became less frequent and the intervals longer. Finally they ceased.

The prayers stopped and were replaced by subdued questions and whispered discussions about the unknown awaiting us outside. After a long time The Chinaman's "all clear" told us it was safe to start home.

It was a little after midnight. The sky was red: the ancient port of Piraeus was burning.

As soon as we got home I fell asleep fully clothed. I slept until a little after three a.m., when a terrific crash shook the whole house, slamming the open windows against their frames. Still groggy, I was dragged out of the house by my mother and once more we were all running for the shelter. The bright glow in the sky cast the shadowed outlines of my fleeing family in sharp relief. We had gone less than a block when an even more ear-splitting thunderclap overtook us. The impact made me stumble but my mother, clutching my hand, did not stop. Lurching on, I had no alternative but to regain my footing. The sky was so luminous I could see Mama's panic-stricken face as clearly as if it were daylight.

Huge, red-hot pieces of metal were raining on the Piraeus area from so great a height that I had to look up to see them. Some seemed to be falling in slow motion. I learned later that a British ship that had blown up, loaded with explosives. Some of the flaming chunks traveled miles before descending and as they hit the ground they caused more fires, adding to the ghastly illumination of the Plain of Attica.

• • •

We spent the rest of the night at the shelter. It had all been too much for a seven-year-old and I slept soundly, perhaps the only one to do so. When morning brought an eerie quiet we returned home slowly and carefully, looking up with apprehension like field mice expecting a hawk to swoop down at any moment from any corner of the sky. Just hours earlier the blazes at Piraeus had set the heavens ashimmer. Now dark smoke hung over us, with a strange smell that would be familiar to me during the next four years. Cordite.

As we later found out, the first wave of planes had dropped magnetic mines at the harbor entrance, trapping the ships. They were followed by screaming Stuka dive bombers, with their gull-shaped wings. The British ship they had hit was the Clan Fraser. Its eruption in turn destroyed eleven more ships, disabled the port, killed hundreds and broke windows over a vast area. (Ours were undamaged because we'd left them open, which reduced the shock.)

The physical devastation was widespread and heartbreaking. The psychological effect was catastrophic. The raid had obliterated any illusions that Greece possessed the realistic capability to tackle this kind of weapons superiority in a straightforward military contest. Overnight a sense of inevitability and resignation had come to permeate everything. My mother lapsed into a constant turmoil of hysteria. Her terror infected the rest of the family, eroding their own efforts to maintain composure. My father came home late every night from The Barracks and, despite his fatigue, devoted long hours trying to allay Mama's fears with soothing words that he perhaps no longer believed. It was to no avail. She repeated incessantly, "The Germans will be here soon. The Germans will be here soon."

The night of Hitler's first air strike had passed, but it had plunged us into a black, black night of the soul. This murk overshadowed every corner of our being. It truly looked so all-encompassing as to be endless.

PART THREE : SHADOWS IN THE DARK

From left: Alexandra, Litsa, Mama, Evangelos, Maria

CHAPTER 13 : *TURNING POINT*

On April 9, 1941, a single blow smashed the delicate shell that surrounded my childhood fantasies. All that I'd taken for granted -- my innocent beliefs, my security -- changed abruptly in a day.

As always now, we went to bed fully dressed in case the Stukas came. That night they didn't, yet something woke me. I raised my head and it took me a few seconds to understand what was happening. My mother lay on her back, moaning with every breath. Her wide eyes looked at the ceiling without expression. My sisters hovered over her, petting her hands and face, pleading with her to say something. She only moaned, stretching her neck as if trying to get up. She was convulsing like a man I'd once seen in a street having an epileptic fit.

I knelt on the bed and took her hand. "Talk to me, Mama! Talk to me, Mama!" She didn't answer. Her face looked strange and her mouth twisted as she tried to say something but failed. Maria ran to the only neighbor who had a telephone and called my father and our doctor. For one moment, evidently exerting supreme effort, my mother managed to lisp a single comprehensible phrase: "My boy... my boy." She was apparently trying to tell my sisters to take care of me. Then she slipped into a coma.

My father arrived. The doctor came, then another, then another. After bending over her a long time they huddled gravely in the hallway with their arms crossed, whispering, nodding or shaking their heads. Ambulances weren't immediately available, being too busy carrying soldiers from the train station to the hospitals, so Mama stayed put for a while. Neighbors came and went all day, some sharing with us what little food they had. I sat on our doorstep or walked aimlessly up and down the street. Finally, after many hours, an ambulance took my parents to the hospital. To me this meant everything would be all right. The doctors and nurses who knew so much would take care of her and she'd soon return. The rest of the day is a blur in my memory. All I recall are somber faces, subdued voices, controlled sobs, and in the distance, sirens and explosions.

• • •

That night I slept with one of my sisters. Mama's big baroque bed was left empty and cold. I awoke when the light was switched on; the blacked-out windows and shutters still sealed us off from the first rays of dawn. My sisters were weeping. At the table where my mother had helped me raise silkworms to teach me to appreciate the wonders of life and creation, my father stood in silence. His eyes told me without words that my mother was dead.

• • •

Alexandra explained to me that Mama had died a few hours before at the hospital. I didn't cry then. My tears flowed only after her funeral, when I was alone. Small though I was, my grief was too intensely personal to expose to well-meaning offers of consolation. I just sat on the edge of the bed as Alexandra spoke, my arms folded. I thought of her face, voice, warmth. How would I get by without her? What would happen to her body when they put her "down there"? Would I be able to communicate with her? Why had she died? Didn't only very old people die? My mother was thirty-eight.

Despite the privacy of my emotions it's hard now to look back and not see how Mama's death reflected the fact that I was, indeed, not alone but very much a child of a community. The funeral was conducted with ancient ceremonies and rituals ingrained into the innermost nature of the Greek people. War or no war, this essential fabric endured. And though the questions about the great mystery of death that now flooded my young mind were specific and personal to me, I came to understand as I grew older that my pain and bewilderment were shared at that time by every sweetheart, mother, father, sister, brother, son, daughter and grandparent whom the war had caused to wear black.

Though still a child, I was beginning to leave my childhood behind, and April 1941 was a turning point in my life. As we were to discover as the month wore on, it was also a turning point for Greece.

• • •

When our shutters were opened that morning golden sunshine and the scent of spring flowers poured in, but these couldn't change the sepulchral atmosphere pervading our house.

My father left to make the funeral arrangements. Our neighbors continued calling. Even people we didn't know came to console and help us. Widows advised my sisters on mourning. Friends and neighbors dug into wardrobes and trunks to bring my sisters black dresses, stockings and shoes. Someone put a black armband on the sleeve of the coat Mama had bought me only a few months before. Our enemies had compelled us to cover our windows with black paper; now this. Blackness was dominating our lives. Everything around me seemed to be dying. Yet this omnipresent blackness had a strangely immunizing effect. When the Luftwaffe sent more of its planes with black crosses to fill our skies, the fear that they evoked shrank in comparison to my family's loss.

The funeral was held that very day in a dim hospital chapel that smelt of stale incense. The many mourners included hospitalized Greek soldiers in pajamas, balancing on crutches. I was barely tall enough to see into the open coffin, which rested on a central pedestal. A green mat covered three wooden steps which everyone climbed to kiss Mama's forehead. My grandmother broke down and was carried out. My turn came. I stood gazing at my mother. Flowers almost filled the coffin. Though beautiful, Mama was very pale, tired and gaunt in her black dress, her lips thin and tight with a blue hue. Cotton protruded from her nostrils. Her clasped fingers bore a small icon of a saint. I kissed her forehead. She was cold as the ice that Mr Stelios, the iceman, left on our steps every summer day. I withdrew to a corner to be alone.

The service was interminable. At last the priest chanted "Eternal be thy memory" three times and crossed himself thrice. Everyone went out. I hid behind a column to see Mama one last time. Stroking her face, I was overcome by a desire to see her as she had been. My thumbs opened her eyelids slowly, exposing eyes like marbles. I realized fully then that I'd never see her again. Closing her eyes gently, I went out. My uncle asked where I'd been and I explained. Terribly upset, he told my father, who looked at me sadly and said, "Leave the boy alone."

• • •

The long journey to the cemetery near Phaleron, by the sea, took the cortege through deserted streets which added to the mood of desolation. The wood-framed hearse, carved with scrolls and angels, was followed by the police chief's limousine. I sat between Mr Archimandritis and his chauffeur. At the graveside the coffin lid was removed for the priest's concluding ceremonies, giving me my final mental picture of Mama. The sealed casket was lowered. Someone gave me a handful of soil to throw on it, like the other mourners. The filling of the grave began and I walked away to the clatter of pebbles on wood. As we proceeded back along the coastal road of Phaleron it was as though the war had grudgingly paused to allow a brief interlude of silence for my mother's farewell and was impatient to resume its tumult, for the sirens now struck up their caterwauling. Explosions boomed from Piraeus in the distance. Hitler's planes were delivering the coup de grace to our defenses there. Our car stopped for a man to emerge from a taxi and position himself on our running board, holding on the window frame as we started moving again.

"What's he doing?" I asked.

"He's the lookout for planes," I was told. "The Germans are shooting at everything moving on this coastal road."

We hadn't got much farther when the lookout man shouted and waved. Planes swooped down and strafed the road. The cars scattered, each to find its own way back to Kallithea through side streets. We arrived home to a crowd of mourners being served coffee and brandy. My sisters had secured a last supply of coffee from Mr Yakoumidis, the plateia coffee-grinder, who was also there paying his respects. It was our last whiff of coffee in our home for years.

And so the day closed, and with it a season in my family's story. It was a day that reflected our community and its moment in time. The men and women milling around me, talking above my head in more than one sense, had gathered to honor one of their own in the house which she had filled with love and the labor of her hands. Not even Hitler, and the imminent dangers that he presented, could keep these Greeks from their parting obligations to their beloved friend as their customs demanded. They'd seen Mama in her roles as mother, wife, neighbor and dutiful citizen. Women like her would keep our community functioning while their menfolk were occupied by the travails of war. It was oddly symbolic that Mama's cortege had been strafed by German bullets, as if the Germans felt that by attacking her funeral procession they could eradicate the indomitable spirit of her kind. Of course they couldn't. And in truth, my mother had succeeded in eluding the Germans, for her haunting dread had been that she would see Nazi conquerors walk our streets. Fate mercifully spared her this awful sight. Too late to inflict more terror on Mama, Hitler's Panzer tanks rolled into Athens seventeen days later.

• • •

My father returned to his post at The Barracks the day after the funeral. He now had many prisoners to process urgently. It was essential to send them to Egypt before the Germans arrived to restore them to our enemies' ranks. My father regarded this mission as gravely important. His sense of duty was always paramount to him, and I came to understand this fully only as I matured.

To augment their mourning wardrobe my sisters went to Mr Spyropoulos' haberdashery and contributed to his thriving business in black dye. Three lively young women became silent black shadows. Their tears did not now flow as easily as before but their anguish was manifest on their ashen faces. I avoided mentioning Mama. Our *Er-Ce-Ah* wasn't permitted to play music, only news broadcasts. These reported that the Germans had taken Belgrade in Yugoslavia and that in North Africa Rommel was about to take Tobruk.

The Stukas came again. And again. And again. We no longer ran to the shelter every time The Chinaman wailed but watched from a window as they screamed toward Piraeus, passing almost over our house. We saw a British Hurricane take on a Stuka, maneuvering nimbly through twists and turns. We heard its machine guns. But an explosion and a column of smoke rising high in the sky told us that the Stuka had succeeded in dropping its deadly load somewhere on the port.

Rumors abounded. "The Yugoslav Army has capitulated." "The Greek Army and the British are retreating." "Nothing can now stop the Germans." We were not only shrouded in darkness of spirit and outlook, but by shadows of uncertainty that clutched at us from within the dark.

Confusion reigned in Kallithea. Looters descended on the bombarded port of Piraeus, emerging with carts of salvage from sunken ships which they hawked in our streets, from tools and pieces of machinery to big burnt lumps of sugar. One neighbor bought a batch of British eyeshields from North Africa and gave me a couple of pairs. Wearing them put me in exalted company, for they would become famously associated with the Desert Fox, Field Marshal Erwin Rommel, leader of Germany's Afrika Corps, who wore them over his peaked cap in preference to heavy German goggles. My grandmother discovered a novel if more mundane way to use them. She wore them when she peeled onions.

• • •

Easter of 1941 came and went without the traditional bells or fireworks. In our house we didn't even notice its passing. I went to The Barracks a few times with my sisters for the food coupons to which the families of Greek officers were entitled. We were supposed to redeem these at nearby military canteens but the shelves were bare and we returned empty-handed.

{ 111 }

The mood of the Italian prisoners had noticeably changed. Basking in the brilliant spring sunshine, they seemed without a care in the world. Not only were they no longer under fire in Albania but word was that they'd soon be liberated by the Germans.

A tall blond prisoner sat alone under a tree, away from the others. He was pointed out to me as a German Stuka pilot who had been shot down. I inspected him from a distance, afraid to approach a member of the horde responsible for our flights to the air raid shelter. But I did have indirect contact with this airman, for my father brought home his confiscated Luger Parabellum pistol, a big, beautiful, shiny weapon which I thought splendid. I was permitted to hold it for a while before it was locked in a drawer, but not without being given a parental lecture about the role of firearms, their appropriate uses, their inappropriate uses and the dangers that dwelt in the exquisite design of some of them, which could so fascinatingly combine the precision of the engineer with the human touch of the craftsman and even the artist. Of course I was too young to take any of this in, at least deeply enough to reflect on it. To me, as it would have been to most little boys, the be-all and end-all of the Luger was that it was a marvelous piece of handiwork that was a joy to behold. Only in later years would I look back on the presence of this weapon under our roof with the thoughtfulness that was its due.

What was really in my father's mind when he brought it into our home? The German company that manufactured Lugers, DWM (Deutsche Waffen und Munitionsfabriken, or the German Weapons and Munitions corporation), had originated in the nineteenth century under the German Empire. Its history was virtually a mirror of the rise of the Reich that was now assailing the rest of Europe. The smooth, excellently-wrought surface of the Luger, and the fine balance of its mechanism, reflected in its way not only the armed might but the very character of contemporary Germany. And yet my father had brought this instrument into our house, to be kept among us. But this icon of a dreaded enemy was surely not just a souvenir to him. He must have been well aware of its portent and overtones. Did he, then, expect to have to use it at some point, in defense of his family? Did he think he would be able to sell it eventually for a sum of money that would be useful to us? Or was there perhaps a deeper psychological meaning to his action? He knew that the Germans were on our doorstep, and that there was nothing he could do about it. Was his personal commandeering of this gun, the signature weapon and emblem of the Nazis racing toward Athens, a response to this knowledge? The Luger stood for everything that was being unleashed against us, including the meticulous exactness and ingenuity with which the Germans pursued their every objective. The fact that my father had this Luger, and was in charge of what became of it and how it was used, could have meant a great deal to him. Did he feel that by placing this one quintessentially German weapon under lock and key, in a place of which he alone was master and of which even Hitler was unaware, he was in some small but symbolically significant way diminishing the Germans' power over, if not Greece, then at least his own spirit?

Whatever the answer, his act of locking the Luger away was not the last of it.

The Deutsche Waffen und Munitionsfabriken had further business with Greece. And with me.

• • •

The Germans seized airfields as they advanced, creating bases from which the Stukas appeared with increasing frequency. Food became even scarcer. Store shelves in Kallithea were now almost empty and the street vendors had disappeared. In the third week of April our *Er-Ce-Ah* announced that the Greek Army had capitulated. With the collapse of Yugoslavia they had been outflanked and the German Panzers had reached Thessaloniki, Greece's second-largest city.

All seemed lost.

• • •

In late April a Greek voice on our *Er-Ce-Ah* announced that the Athens radio service was about to cease being Greek as it was about to be taken over by the Germans. Listeners were advised to give no credence to what was broadcast in future.

"The struggle will continue elsewhere," the voice said. "Long live Greece!"

And it went off the air.

I was sitting on our front steps that afternoon when a taxi pulled up and my uniformed father stepped out. I was surprised to see him so early. I followed him into the house where my sisters and I gathered around him. He hung up his military cap and told us, "It's all over. The Germans are in Athens." Without another word he went to the bedroom, took off his uniform and hung it in his big walnut wardrobe.

He never wore it again.

• • •

We learned later that my father had arrived at The Barracks that morning to find total confusion.

The German mechanized forces at that time at the gates of Athens. The British, Australians and New Zealanders who'd been in Athens to help us were scrambling to any port they could find to escape to Crete or Egypt.

Athens had been declared an open city, meaning it would no longer be defended. This was to avoid pointless bloodshed and destruction. The staff of The Barracks went home. My father was the last to leave, his sense of duty keeping him at his post as the sole guard of hundreds of Italians and some German prisoners. He was armed with a rifle. He finally realized the absurdity and futility of the situation and thought of what might happen to his children if he were captured.

Taking as many documents as he could, he found a taxi and came home.

• • •

On entering Athens the Germans were quick to emblazon their presence upon the greatest and most visible icon of Greece and the values that Greeks had given western civilization. We heard a commotion outside and found that our neighbors were abuzz as news of this action circulated. We climbed the wrought-iron stairs to our terrace to see for ourselves. There, on the south side of our holy rock, the Acropolis, beside the Parthenon, a huge hung unfurled. Through my father's binoculars I recognized the image which, ironically, I had first seen on March 25, Greece's Independence Day.

The flag was red with a black stripe, a white circle in the center, and inside that circle a black crooked cross.

The creeping spider had arrived.

Evangelos' father and the life-saving roof garden. It was from this vantage point that the movements of the Luftwaffe were watched.

The summer of '41 brought what the Germans announced as a "new order". It was made clear that Greeks would have to obey the invaders if they knew what was good for them.

Greece adapted, but not as the Germans wanted. The Occupation was a reality that Greeks had to accept if they were to survive. Besides, they were too stunned and drained to do otherwise. But accepting military and political facts doesn't necessarily mean servility, and if the Germans expected a slave mentality in their new subjects they were mistaken.

From the day they arrived the Nazis were resisted, both psychologically and practically. For most Greeks, devoid of material means to fight, resistance could be no more than a private sense of rebellion, derived at least in part, perhaps, from an ancient awareness of the indestructibility of their people. But these reserves of defiance were interwoven with exhaustion, fear and knowledge of the armed might that Hitler had at his disposal.

In parallel with this spirit of rebellion simmering just under the surface came action of a decidedly deadly nature. The armed Greek Resistance fought the invaders tooth and nail. Some took to the mountains immediately to organize outposts from which the enemy could be harassed. Others continued their seemingly innocuous lives in villages, towns and cities. Outwardly they were ordinary people going about their routine business. They represented no particular social class or economic level. They were shopkeepers, tram conductors, students and a host of other anonymous toilers in the obscure corners of everyday life. Secretly, with scant resources and in constant peril, they led double lives and worked to make the Germans pay dearly for invading our country.

Some of these heroes belonged to my family's world and their faces are etched in my memory. Among them were Manolis Glezos and Apostolos Santas whose courage and audacity inspired not only Greeks but people across occupied Europe. On May 30, 1941, they scaled the sheer walls of the Acropolis and took down the hated swastika flag under the eyes of the German guards.

Not all resistance actions could be so conspicuous. There were innumerable small acts of resistance, each of which on its own tended not to inflict massive damage on the Nazi infrastructure but only dented it. But through the accumulated effects of this tireless campaign of retaliation, constantly eroding and incrementally chipping away at the structures and arrogance that underlay the Nazi presence, Greeks made it impossible for the invaders to rest as easily in Greece as they would have liked. Hitler's forces were continually reminded that they were in a country that did not want them.

On one hand there were the Greeks who were dedicated to working persistently against the occupiers in countless practical ways, involving militant action. On the other hand there were those whose rejection of the Nazis was firm and steady but quiet. These were men and women whose family obligations precluded them from taking to the hills or joining in midnight raids, but who nevertheless supported the spirit of the Resistance as best as they could.

One of these patriots was my father.

• • •

It might have been wiser for my father to comply meekly with the Occupation. His children had just lost a mother. Losing a father as well would have been a disaster for us that can hardly be described. Being arrested by the Germans meant death, perhaps also torture. But as I've explained, duty was dear to my father, and his conception of his duty to

{ 118 }

his family was so bound up with his idea of duty to his country that the two were inseparable in his mind.

The Germans imposed many restrictions. One was a curfew which changed from time to time during the Occupation, ranging from early evening to midnight. All transportation ceased at the stipulated hour, after which the streets emptied except for the footfalls of patrolling soldiers and the occasional rumble of their vehicles. All firearms had to be surrendered; the penalty for possessing one after the deadline was death.

Among these edicts was a proclamation that all radios had to be taken to designated places to be adjusted so that they would receive only the Nazi-run radio station in Athens. After this adjustment was made, the radios were sealed. Anyone who tampered with the seal or failed to submit their radio for adjustment faced imprisonment, banishment to a German concentration camp or even execution.

Despite this terrible risk, my father chose not to take our *Er-Ce-Ah* in to be given the Nazi treatment. He decided that he would obediently surrender the Luger pistol he'd confiscated from the German pilot but he drew the line at letting them muzzle the radio that provided us with our precious lifeline of Allied war news.

As with so much that happened during those years, I was later to see a greater significance in these events than my childish mind could discern at the time. With hindsight I am sure that my father was conscious of the counterbalance and proportion of his decision to keep the radio while yielding the gun. It reflected an exchange with the Germans that was both rational and honorable. Giving up the Luger was an acknowledgement of the brute fact that the Germans were at that point masters of armed power in Greece. If indeed my father had seen his secret retention of the pistol as a kind of defiance of this fact of superior German force, he now recognized that his action had by this time acquired a weight of risk too great for a responsible family man to bear. Still, it must have been difficult for him to unlock that drawer, remove the Luger, look at for the last time in its capacity as his personal possession, and then take it to surrender to the German authorities.

The radio was another matter. While it, too, was a mechanism, it was also more than that. It was the bringer of morale, of hope, of free information without which the human soul could not endure. And so as I grew up I would come to look back to this decision of my father's as a record of his priorities and values, and of his belief that while bullets were powerful, and were to be avoided because they could rend flesh and bone, it was even more important to avoid the rending of the spirit that came from being deprived of ideas and information. And the risks that he took in keeping the radio would prove to be no less dangerous than the risk he had quelled by agreeing to surrender the Luger.

But my father's defiance of the radio censorship law was far from being the only source of our worries for his safety. Less than a week after the Germans entered Athens, our doorbell rang. My sister Maria opened it to see armed Italian soldiers filling two small gray-green trucks. An officer asked for my father and ordered him to accompany them immediately.

We watched as he was escorted into a truck and driven away.

• • •

Days passed and became weeks without any news. We were frantic. We had no idea of his whereabouts. We had no idea whether this was somehow connected with his possession of the Luger. Had they imprisoned him? Executed him? Sent him to a concentration camp? We had no money. All we had to eat was some pasta and beans that our provident mother had stored in the sofa-trunk for emergencies. Our efforts to find information were in vain.

Maria and I were in Athens one day trying to learn anything we could about our father's fate when we chanced on a German mechanized convoy on Stadiou Street, one of the main thoroughfares.

Anyone who saw this parade could be forgiven for thinking that no force on earth could prevail against the Reich. I had never seen anything like it, even in pictures. It was an intimidating and overwhelming sight even to adults but especially to a child. A procession of monstrous tanks marked with the black cross rumbled thunderously by on the clanking plates of their caterpillar tracks. The huge cannon barrels, looming awesomely from the metal bulk of the juggernauts, projected an inhuman power of threat and destruction that widened my eyes and stilled the crowd. Soldiers wearing black berets and earphones protruded from the tops of the vehicles amid arrays of antennae. Steel-helmeted men with rifles clamped between their knees filled the benches of truck after truck. Mesmerized, I stepped unthinkingly from the sidewalk into the path of an approaching motorcycle with sidecar. Maria wrenched me back just in time as the motorcyclist slammed on his brakes.

As if this pageant of German might were insufficient, the Luftwaffe provided with a spectacular air show on an ongoing basis. The area of Kalamaki, where the Germans had taken over an airfield, was a few miles out of Athens. The air space over our neighborhood happened to be where the planes began reducing altitude to land. The sight of the enemy aircraft descending over our streets and rooftops no doubt chilled my elders, but to a little boy it was enthralling.

In the third week of May German paratroopers were dropped on the island of Crete, which was still being defended by Greek and Allied soldiers and local civilians. We learned of this battle from the newspapers and our now illegal *Er-Ce-Ah*. The fighting on Crete raged until around the end of the month and during this period our terrace was a ringside seat from which I followed with fascination the everlasting stream of

Junkers Ju 52 transport planes that came and went directly over our house. Their corrugated plating gave them a wrinkled appearance that was very distinctive.

Ground fire in Crete left some of these aircraft with gaping holes in their fuselage, dead propellers or smoking engines. Only as an adult would I discover that in viewing this panorama I was witnessing history in the making. This was not just because of the historic nature of the war in general but because although the Germans had used paratroopers before, the Crete campaign was the first time they were used as the main thrust of a large-scale attack. Britain was to increase its paratrooper force as a result and airborne commandos became an increasingly important part of its military.

Although the Germans managed to take Crete, it was by no means the relatively painless victory they'd expected. They were particularly shocked by the ferocity with which the civilian population – men, women and children – rose up against them with a united fury that was unprecedented in the Germans' experience of the countries they'd thus far invaded. Nor did their problems cease once they established themselves on the island. It was if all the fury of the suppressed Greek mainland had been channeled to one spot.

Crete was not to be easy for the Germans.

• • •

Our terrace didn't only give me a daily spectacle of German air power and a window on the damage that the enemy's planes were receiving on their forays to Crete: my special and privileged position also enabled me to monitor the doings on our street before anyone else in the house, like a sailor surveying the horizon from a crow's nest high above his shipmates. On one of the days when I was on our terrace watching planes, I heard a vehicle draw up below. Looking over the parapet I saw an Italian truck, small and gray-green like the ones that had taken my father away. Two Italian soldiers jumped out from the back, followed by my father. They unloaded a few cardboard boxes on the sidewalk and left. I ran down to greet him with my sisters. After an emotional embrace we carried the boxes inside and gathered around the table where my father told us his story.

Because of his position at The Barracks, he'd been taken for interrogation to the Greek city of Corinth, some fifty miles from Athens, where an Italian headquarters had been set up under Germany's wing. There my father was questioned about his work. Since he'd been privy to no military secrets, and his duties had mainly involved harmless Red Cross matters regarding prisoners of war, he had no qualms about telling them everything he knew, which he patiently did.

There was one major problem. Of the thousands of Italian prisoners he'd overseen, a single one saw fit to accuse my father of mistreating prisoners. This charge carried internment in Italy or death. Who was the accuser? None other than Mario, the fascist Blackshirt who'd sung "Sucker Mussolini" so willingly to entertain us.

Fortunately Mario stood alone in his complaint. The Italian officers who'd worked under him rose to his defense. He had, they asserted, not only treated all the prisoners according to the Geneva Convention, but had gone well beyond those requirements and had behaved as a gentleman, treating each of the men in his charge with respect. In their gratitude to him these officers of Italy successfully countered their own countryman's malicious charge so that my father, their former jailer, could be restored to his family. To underline their high regard for him, they didn't turn him loose empty-handed but delivered him to our door accompanied by the boxes I'd seen being unpacked from the truck. In them we discovered canned food, hardtack crackers and parmesan cheese. Though not much, it was enough to make a difference to our diet. But of far greater importance was that even the enemies of my country that little stockpile exceeded the riches of Aladdin's Cave.

• • •

In the tradition of the Orthodox Church, a bereavement is marked by a memorial service after forty days. My mother's was now held. It seemed to me like a milder version of the funeral and it reopened emotional wounds that had just begun to heal. Once again well-wishers streamed to our house to offer condolences, led by the mayor of Kallithea, Mr Arapakis. It was customary to toast the deceased with a glass of brandy and a cup of coffee. We could still offer everyone a small Metaxa brandy but coffee was a luxury of the past.

A lack of coffee wasn't the worst of our problems. Like other families, we were running out of food. One solution in our neighborhood was to grow vegetables, but our small, shady garden wasn't suited to this, so my father came up with a plan. He set us to work scouring the area for every discarded tin can or other container we could find, some from a German camp near the cemetery where my mother lay. These we filled with soil and put them in the only place that had full sunlight: our terrace.

My contribution didn't stop there. Armed each day with a small bucket, dustpan and broom, I was assigned to wander the streets collecting fresh donkey and horse manure for fertilizer. I felt demeaned in the eyes of my peers, some of whom were highly amused to see me rounding up droppings and had no hesitation in loudly expressing their mirth as I went about my chores. But I had the last laugh, for our terrace garden grew so well over the long summer months that envious neighbors were soon calling it the Hanging Gardens of Babylon. The observation post from which I viewed the Luftwaffe's movements thus acquired an additional new role as our source of nourishment, and we thankfully harvested such welcome crops as tomatoes and eggplant. Alas, my sisters had to cook it all without our accustomed olive oil, which was no longer

{ 124 }

to be found. Also, our diet would have been better if we had been able to plant potatoes, but no potatoes could be found anywhere for seed. Potatoes just passed out of everyone's vocabulary.

Despite our determined efforts, the terrace garden wasn't productive enough to feed us. My father began to sell possessions like jewelry and heirlooms, some of which had been in our family for generations. The money that this raised bought a few gallons of olive oil on the black market, as well as a few other staples that kept us going a while longer.

Just barely.

• • •

And so the summer of 1941 passed into the pages of the history books.

Children are blessed with the ability to enter worlds of imagination that can distract them from the evils of reality, and much of the time my games distracted me from the things that my growing mind was coming to understand about our circumstances. I was, after all, a little boy, and a good deal of my days was a tapestry of hide-and-seek, marbles and let's-pretend-we're-people-in-the-movies. On wings of fancy I could soar away into realms of make-believe where neither Germans nor Italians nor hunger pangs could touch me. In all ways that mattered I was lord of the streets that I roamed in search of mischief.

But there was one game I now avoided. It was when we formed a circle and recited a Greek children's rhyme:

Fine salt,
Rock salt,
I lost my mother
and I am looking for her.

Yaya and the apple of her eye on the front steps of the house in Kallithea

My father's disposal of our jewelry and heirlooms bought us groceries for another month at most. By the fall of 1941 it had become quite apparent that we couldn't survive under these conditions. We had nothing more to sell or barter. The gloom in our house steadily deepened. Then a partial salvation arrived in the unexpected form of my Uncle Alfredos.

Formerly a judge on the island of Kerkyra (Corfu), Uncle Alfredos had been drafted at the outbreak of the war. He was now demobilized and serving as a justice of the peace in the rural village of Leonidion on the Peloponnese peninsula, where food was more readily available. It was decided that the most vulnerable members of our family -- my grandmother, my sister Alexandra and I -- would go to live with him. A few months earlier Alexandra had developed pleurisy, a painful inflammation of the lining of the lungs and chest, which had left her weak. Three relatives were as many as Uncle Alfredos could take in. My father and my two other sisters stayed behind in Kallithea to take their chances.

To make the trip we had to apply to the occupation authorities for travel documents, so Alexandra and I went to the plateia to have our pictures taken for identity cards. I sat very still on a chair in the open air and stared at the black lens of the camera. When my picture had been taken there in times past my mother's happy face had been behind the photographer's as she told me how to pose, with my sisters and an inevitable circle of other children gleefully enjoying the sight of my subjection to the embarrassing rigmarole. Now only the familiar photographer with the caved-in cheeks and doleful face was there and he went mechanically through the process of taking and developing our pictures. Gone were the vendors who had sold children peanuts in small paper cones for pennies. The previously lively, gurgling water fountain in the center of the plateia was dry and silent. The place was deserted.

• • •

My uncle, my grandmother, Alexandra and I left the following day carrying our belongings in a few bundles tied with string. We took the streetcar to a part of Athens from where a bus service ran to the town of Nauplion. As there was no highway to Leonidion we were to travel by boat the rest of the way.

Buses were the most common form of public transport then. From the beginning of the German Occupation until the end of the war there was little or no gasoline for public transport in Greece. Gasoline in occupied countries was commandeered by the Germans. The few buses serving the Athens area were thus modified to burn wood. The result was an extraordinary vehicle called a *gazozen* (a word of French origin), which had a chimney. The furnace was a large cylinder bolted to the back of the bus next to a bin of firewood. Wood was fed through an opening in the top of the cylinder until it was full, then an airtight lid was shut. The cylinder was heated underneath with more firewood and the temperature raised with hand-cranked bellows. All this produced a combustible if poor-quality gas which was piped into the engine, propelling the bus at twenty miles an hour or so. The bus stopped periodically for the conductor and passengers to take turns cranking the bellows for five or ten minutes to generate more gas. If the cylinder needed more wood it would take much longer to get going again.

The *gazozen* bus we took with Uncle Alfredos was a small, rickety old thing made mostly of plywood on a Ford truck frame. It could hold about twenty people. We had to go via Corinth on a narrow road that followed the coastline, sometimes along precipitous cliffs. The *gazozen* crawled at an agonizingly slow pace, stopping at checkpoints where German soldiers scrutinized us and the bus, inspected our papers and poked our bundles.

After many hours we reached Kaki Skala ("Bad Pass"), a few miles from Corinth. The old road had been cut through the rock. The sheer cliff dropped straight into the sea. Here our *gazozen* gasped its last and had to have its firewood replenished. The passengers, numb from the long, arduous trip in the bone-rattling machine, disembarked with relief. We walked around or sat down contemplating the blue sea that simmered in the midday sun. I sat on the stone parapet gnawing a piece of dry bread under the watchful eyes of my grandmother, who had produced this morsel from a clean, folded towel as a surprise.

As in many other things, Alexandra was well versed in Greek mythology and as I ate she told me that Theseus, the hero of ancient Greek legend and slayer of the monster called the Minotaur, had passed this very way on his adventures. According to tradition it was here that he'd slain the evil Skiron, who used to waylay travelers and throw them over the cliff to their deaths. I was enthralled by her tale of another of Theseus's foes, the wicked giant Procrustes, who put his victims on a special bed and if their legs happened to be longer than the bed, Procrustes would cut them off; if they were shorter, he'd stretch the prisoner to fit. I imagined Theseus as bigger than any German soldier, armed with a shiny sword of justice. My excitement was undiminished by the fact that I was listening to these glorious fables and dreaming my dreams while looking upon a mouse-colored, decrepit old Ford bus with a party of desperate men cranking away to revitalize it so we could get back on the road.

• • •

We finally reached the Corinth Canal. The big bridge spanning it had been blown up by the retreating British. We approached the east entrance to the canal via a temporary dirt road where the banks sloped gently into the sea. The bus stopped there for some time. A temporary pontoon bridge, built by the Germans, was guarded lazily by a few Italian soldiers, most of them just resting on the pebbled beach. We waited there for a couple of hours because endless convoys of German military vehicles were crossing, laden with soldiers and equipment. Eventually they gave us the go-ahead. We crossed and continued our slow, tiresome journey on the Peloponnese peninsula toward the city of Argos, which in ancient times had rivaled Sparta. Along the road were burnt-out hulks of British trucks and equipment, one or two with shreds of bloody uniforms. Occasionally we passed long lines of ragged British prisoners marching in the opposite direction. We learned that terrible battles between the Germans and the retreating British had been fought nearby.

And so we came to the port of Nauplion, which for a short time had been the first capital of modern Greece when the country gained independence from the Turks in the early nineteenth century. The Venetians of centuries past had left their stamp in the narrow streets and Italianesque buildings. We spent a day or two there. The Palamidi, the prison-citadel, loomed high above the town. I was hungry and relished a bit of thick condensed milk from a Red Cross can. Germans in field-gray uniforms and steel helmets were everywhere. I glanced at them furtively, afraid to meet their eyes. Bedraggled British prisoners with dirty faces and matted hair sat around looking forlorn. Tied-up boats rocked gently in calm blue water. A German sentry with a rifle paced, his jackboots clanking on the cobblestones. Some boys bent over the quay, looking into the sea. One dangled a string in the water, moving it back and forth. I knelt to peer into the shallow clear waters: rifles were piled up like matchsticks at the bottom, stretching out as far as I could see. The British had dumped their Lee-Enfield rifles after removing the bolt to make them inoperable.

The "fishing" boy, aged fourteen or so, would deftly grapple a rifle with a hook at the end of his string, pull his catch up, examine it, take a few imaginary shots into the sky, then toss it back in. I was fascinated. The sentry paused occasionally to see that every rifle found its way back to the bottom to await eventual collection by the Wermacht.

• • •

In late morning we boarded a *venzina*, a sturdy, open, diesel-powered water taxi that ferried us to Leonidion. This craft was relatively small; I could touch the water. In the front, near the pilot, I stood on a bench while Alexandra kept a protective hand on me in the gently swaying motion. A dozen or so passengers crammed the deck, some sitting on their belongings. I drained my condensed milk can and threw it in the sea. Our voyage seemed to last for hours. At length our destination took shape on the horizon. As if through a zoom lens, Leonidion grew bigger and clearer in a smoothly unhurried motion. This image of the end of our journey growing nearer and nearer and larger and larger, as we chugged steadily through the placid waters, was imprinted indelibly on my mind. Neither the passage of years nor any other event of my life has erased or altered it. I'm glad. I don't want to forget the time I spent in Leonidion. There I was embraced in a carefree environment that allowed me, all too briefly, to be not a child of the war but simply a little boy again.

CHAPTER 16 : *A THOUSAND CUPS OF COFFEE*

Coming into port, our captain deftly avoided the wreck of a very large fishing boat that lay semi-submerged in the middle of the little harbor. "The Stukas got it," he remarked. "It was the Aghia Varvara with twenty Greek and English soldiers. Fortunately they heard the Stuka coming and scrambled out just in time and were saved."

A mole -- a wall in the sea – protected the port. From part of its bulk arose the customs house, where the chief customs officer lived. He was a gracious host and we stayed with him until a horse-drawn cart was found for us. Our bundles were piled on it, with my grandmother and I perched on top, and Alexandra and Uncle Alfredos walked alongside as we made our way down the tree-lined road into the village of Leonidion. It was September, 1941. Until the summer of 1942 this would be my world. It was also the world of a Greece that had existed before the Germans came and would persist through the war despite the bombs and all that they brought with them.

• • •

The authorities had assigned a house to my uncle as part of his position as the new judge, but as it wasn't yet ready we spent a few nights at the only inn. It was on a side street off the winding main road that traversed the village, following the river in varying proximity. The inn, beside the ruins of a Venetian tower, was run by a short, amiable lady everybody called Mrs Sophia. (Greek custom permits the title with the first name, simultaneously affording familiarity and respect.) Her smiling husband was Pavlos. We had our first proper meal in a

{ 133 }

month at the little coffee shop on the local plateia. The rest of the evening I explored.

The village lay in a small valley. Half the mountain on your right, as you faced the town, had slid down along its fault line exposing a vertical wall of red earth, naked except for a few bushes sprouting from crags, defying gravity and the elements. The red earth stopped at a ridge where trees and brush began.

The other half of the mountain spilled gently into the valley, with small white houses spreading down to a wide river. In summer this river dried up to expose a bed of large polished stones interspersed with brush and ancient olive and plane trees. In winter this bed became the watery outlet of the mountains of the province of Arcadia; then it was to be feared. A solitary bridge spanned it from the town, allowing the public road, as it was called, to continue on to the neighboring port village of Plaka.

The other side of the river sloped up the smaller mountain, topped by a little church of the prophet Elias, whose contemplative retreat to the high crags was commemorated by many Greek mountaintop churches in his name. Plane trees and twisted olive trees grew everywhere. Some of the olive trees were immense and it was said they went back to the time when Christ had walked the earth. The shore area, Lakos ("Dip"), was replete with citrus orchards.

Our house became available. It was near the plateia, on a creek amid olive trees with banks of wild flowers and other aromatic plants. You crossed the creek on a small concrete bridge. Half a dozen irregularly shaped granite boulders had rolled down the mountain and stuck out of the ground like a dragon's teeth.

The house, a few hundred years old, looked bigger than its two stories, perhaps because it had apparently been built as a stronghold against Turks or marauding pirates from the region of Africa once called the Barbary Coast. Its walls were almost one and a half feet thick, the lower windows barricaded by hefty wrought iron bars outside and massive wooden shutters within. The high wall around the abundant garden had a huge wooden gate with history written into its unpainted, weathered surface. It looked as if it had been sandblasted at some point, exposing every detail of its grain. Its key was enormous and must have weighed over a pound. Two stout bars strengthened it further to withstand ramming.

There was a door at ground level but the main entrance, reached by broad stone steps, was on the upper story where we had our bedrooms, a spacious salon and a smaller room which became our winter headquarters since it had the only fireplace. Downstairs were the dining room, spare room and kitchen. The only internal passage between the two levels was via a trapdoor and very steep stairs. My heavy-set grandmother used the outside steps in all weather.

By the gate a tiled roof covered a substantial former stable that served as both woodshed and our only toilet. Our water was rain which the gutters deposited into an ample stone cistern. The locals claimed that many years before, eels had been put in the cisterns to devour insects. For months I lay on the cistern peering through the opening for an eel. The experience triggered a train of philosophical reflection in me: I concluded that people saw what they wished and that much of which they spoke existed only in their imaginations, including gremlins, ghosts and perhaps even the God who had taken my mother; at least as my elders described Him.

• • •

My sister began her last year of secondary education at the local school, the Gymnasion, whose few students were mostly from well-to-do homes. My elementary school was on the main road to Plaka, just before the bridge over the river. It was an attractive building with a play area. I was now in the second grade. My teacher, a kind young man in his twenties, was known (like Mrs Sophia at the inn) by a title of respect followed by his first name; we called him Kyrios Kostas (Mr Kostas). Unlike the rather authoritarian teachers I'd known, he was loving, and loved in return by all. I settled in well and soon became known as a bright pupil. I made friends: our neighbor Giorgos; Diamanto, daughter of Mrs Metaxia, a poor widow who wove carpets and raised vegetables and whose son entertained passersby with beautiful singing; Marigoula, daughter of the widower Dr Merikakis, one of the town's two physicians; Demos, whose father owned the coffee shop.

My uncle swiftly established his position as justice of the peace. I attended several sessions in the small courtroom where he settled local disputes. Because of the astronomical inflation and the impoverishment of the government, public officials were partly paid by a custom whereby, as a kind of tax, portions of olive oil and other goods from the area's producers were withheld and given to public officials in lieu of money. I heard many a poor farmer grumble about it. Uncle Alfredos also received "presents of appreciation": a sack of flour, fruit, a chicken and the like. Although this system kept us reasonably well-fed by 1941 standards, I went to bed many times with only a bowl of gruel in my belly. Yet this was often more than my family in Athens had.

• • •

The mild Mediterranean evenings encouraged outdoor socializing. Even on winter evenings people gathered in Leonidion's plateia which, with its coffee shop was the social hub, as it was and still is in many a Greek village. Men, women and children dressed for the occasion. For men it was a particularly important forum. They congregated there to play cards, debate philosophy and politics, gossip, bemoan the state of the world, commiserate about the injustices visited on them, vent outrage against their personal enemies or politicians who displeased them, describe their small personal triumphs, consult one another on the afflictions of the body, and much more, while endlessly sipping small cups of strong black coffee or carbonated drinks. Coming after our coffee famine in Kallithea, the supply of coffee seemed bountiful to the point of luxury. To a child's eyes it appeared that a thousand cups of precious coffee were poured and drunk at each of these assemblies.

The war inevitably featured in the wide-ranging conversations, but the function of these gatherings transcended the news of the day. In some ways they were the heart of all that is Greek, and unquestionably my brightest moments in Leonidion were experienced during those evenings on the plateia. They were an inexhaustible theater of drama, comedy and humanity. When I tired of playing by myself or with other children I roosted on a chair to observe the adults and listen to their stories. Sitting there nightly in the open air until very late in the mild evenings under the stars I eventually got to know the entire village. The evenings began a little before sunset. The villagers ambled to the plateia alone or with their families, greeted one another courteously, and found their seats. By dusk every table was taken. Sparse light came from within the café and then, when the village's generator was turned off after 11 p.m. or even earlier for lack of fuel, from kerosene lamps.

Regular patrons saw all their fellow villagers there: the big, handsome schoolteacher Mimis Kozakos, with dark, curly hair; the self-assured lawyer Nikos Mavrakis, a politically informed man of high intellect with a gift for gab and a fund of fascinating stories; the customs official with his small son; the agricultural expert with his wife and their little daughter Ermione; Nikos the pharmacist; Mr Rigos the banker; Mr Zouvas the gendarmerie captain, who was in charge of keeping the peace in a town where the peace never seemed to be disturbed (save perhaps for the occasional missing chicken), and many more. I especially looked forward to the presence of the telegrapher, Mr Salahas, because of his Russian wife Sonia, who spoke Greek with an exotic accent. She could have qualified as a model for the painter Rubens, known for his voluptuous female figures, and I secretly admired her ample figure and décolletage with tremendous interest.

The cast of characters who came and went in the evening light of the plateia would populate my imagination and haunt my memories for a lifetime. If any of these remarkable individuals stands out with special vividness it is probably Byron, the tall and flamboyant village crier with his copious handlebar moustache. An independent spirit, he never hesitated to voice his opinions even when they were sure to raise eyebrows. There was uncertainty as to his real name. It was said he had arrived in Leonidion in the nineteen-twenties, impeccably and expensively dressed, flaunting a bulky bankroll. Because of his lordly generosity and dazzling appearance the locals dubbed him "Lord Byron", after the colorful English poet. After a while his money evaporated, as did much of his mystique as well as the title "Lord", but the name "Byron" stuck. He became the community's crier, grandly announcing important events, informing the public about the reward for a farmer's lost cow, and so on. Once, when his purse and belly were both empty, he took to the streets bellowing in a stentorian voice, "Whoever is hungry, come tonight and have dinner at Byron's house. Don't forget to bring some food with you." This creative ploy secured him a few square meals from the amused villagers. His wit and resourcefulness never let him down. Like so many of his neighbors, he was a survivor.

• • •

Although Leonidion was for a time my refuge from the war, the events crowding in on Greece were always present. It was on one of those evenings at the plateia, borne away by the never-ending stream of talk that swirled about me, that I heard of a large group of British and Greek soldiers who had hidden around the port of Plaka while seeking a boat to the southern part of the Peloponnese peninsula from where they could be evacuated by the British fleet to Egypt. The Germans spotted them from the air and dispatched Stukas to wipe them out. But a Greek officer who was fluent in German got on a field radio – a portable transmitter and receiver -- and gave the planes the wrong coordinates. As a result they dropped their bombs on the orchards in Lakos. Many citrus trees were destroyed but the soldiers were saved.

And so the days and weeks went by with a normality that I hadn't known for over a year. Going to school, playing with friends, exploring, climbing the age-old olive trees, chasing cicadas, and being accepted as a member of the village. In the latter we were helped greatly by Uncle Alfredos' social status as a judge. In those days there was a definite dividing-line between the intelligentsia and the ordinary hard-working people who formed the backbone of the country. Usually people of special status, like my uncle, sat together at one or two central tables on the plateia while lesser inhabitants sat at the periphery. This social order also manifested itself in the patronizing manner of many of the community's leaders and the ingratiating demeanor of many of the common folk in the presence of their "betters". Small as I was, it wasn't lost on me how obsequiously some people approached our table to introduce themselves to my uncle.

Alexandra and I shared the limelight of our relative's rank and were perceived as being from the glamorous big city of Athens. In time, however, this superficial distinction receded and the villagers became fond of us for our own sakes. Alexandra was admired for her seriousness, obvious intelligence, striking appearance and impressive manner. As for me, bright children always attract attention. I was asked time and again to perform for my elders by reading the newspaper aloud or reciting poetry. I was far from falsely modest and enjoyed the flattering applause, but in private I wondered why they made so much fuss over something so simple.

Only when I grew up and had children of my own would I realize that in frightening times nothing gives an adult hope as much as the promise of a child.

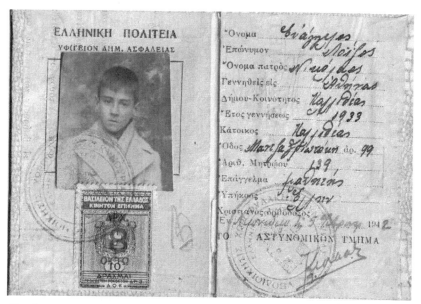

ID document to travel in occupied Greece.

Evangelos with Alexandra (top right) and some of her school
friends in Leonidion.

CHAPTER 17 : *REUNIONS*

One day a new relative arrived at the Leonidion house: Aunt Koula, my uncle's wife. It was a moving reunion. They'd been married only a few months when he was drafted and they hadn't seen each other since. She was a teacher from the island of Kerkyra where Uncle Alfredos had previously been a judge. She began teaching the third grade at the village school and she added a new nuance to the female presence that my grandmother and Alexandra had established in my uncle's house. The gloom that had pervaded my mind since my mother's death dissipated, visiting me now only at night when I lay alone in bed watching the flickering shadows cast by the smoky kerosene lamp. Sometimes after the lamp was extinguished, shadows of another kind flitted through my mind until I fell asleep. But on the whole I was becoming used to my new life.

I liked it.

• • •

Occasionally we received letters from Kallithea. These were always carefully written to avoid any mention of hardship at home. It was remarkable that mail reached us at all. The government postal service had stopped. Mail was delivered by traders who traveled around doing business in foodstuffs and carried letters on the side for a small fee. They didn't deliver to homes but established a base where you'd have to go periodically to fetch mail and give them letters you wanted them to deliver to anyone on their route. Leonidion's mail base was the plateia, where our courier, Pantelis, added to his mail-delivery function the role of general news-bringer. Until late at night, over many cups of coffee, he would tell his mail clients the latest from Athens about the famine or the war. Sometimes he augmented his reports with stories of his own wartime experience in Albania a short time before. One night he told us how he'd fought the Italians on those snowy mountains and how, in a charge, with no ammunition left, he'd bayoneted his opponent.

"I still remember the look in his eyes when I did it. Oh God, how I wish none of this had happened! He must have had a mother, wife and children too." He became silent. It was hard to visualize the mild-mannered Pantelis in such a bloody situation.

• • •

A month or so after our coming to Leonidion a news flash rippled through the village: "The Italians are here!"

The German High Command had designated the Peloponnese region an Italian sphere of operations. I raced with my friends to the dry riverbed and there sat about fifty Italian soldiers and their officer, resting on stones beside their gear and rifles. I had seen large numbers of Italians as prisoners at The Barracks, but this was the first group of this size I'd seen as conquerors, albeit on the heels of the real conquerors, their German allies. They looked like the prisoners I'd known but were more confident and in much better shape, with more complete uniforms.

Later that day this Italian unit requisitioned a house on the main road, the home of Mrs Stella Kambysi. Here they hoisted their red, white and green flag, the Tricolore. Then they promptly withdrew into the house and, except for their commander, almost never came out. Though their presence was felt, it was unobtrusive.

Their commander, Monti, a well-mannered, handsome blond man in his thirties, treated everyone courteously. A villager, Mr Sorras, owned a fine horse, and Monti asked him to allow him to ride it in the evenings. Mr Sorras, a successful merchant with a walrus moustache, gave his consent, either because he knew he really had no choice or because he wanted to ingratiate himself. Whatever the reason, we soon became used to the sight of Monti astride his mount trotting along the main street of Leonidion on his way to Lakos, politely greeting all prominent citizens he came across.

Beneath Monti's courtliness, it turned out, a dark secret festered: he had syphilis. Since his unit had no doctor, he asked one the village's two physicians, Dr Merikakis, to administer the injections of the drug Salvarsan that he needed to treat his embarrassing condition. Dr Merikakis complied, but decided that doctor-patient confidentiality didn't apply to the enemy. Soon the whole village knew the intimate details of Monti's affliction. The information may have prompted smirks but it also caused Alexandra some distress. One evening, mounted on Mr Sorras' stallion, Monti encountered our family out walking. Debonair as ever, he greeted everyone and, leaning down from his steed, gently shook Alexandra's hand. She reciprocated cordially in fluent Italian, but after he'd proceeded on his way she shuddered and rushed back to our house where she repeatedly washed her hands for fear that the syphilis spirochetes had penetrated his gloved hand and infected her.

• • •

The autumn of 1941 gave way to a winter whose first months were quite mild and barely altered our outdoor lifestyle. Our evenings on the plateia continued, as did Monti's nightly parade in the street on his way to Lakos. His men went on maintaining their low profile, rarely venturing beyond the perimeter of their billet. There were rumors of Greek Resistance units forming in the mountains. One day, during my usual escapades in the river area looking for lizards and snakes, I found a small cache of rifle ammunition and a hand grenade hidden under a rock, which I brought home and exhibited triumphantly. To my annoyance, my shaken family took them away and disposed of them at some unknown spot where I could never find them again.

With the psychological pressures of the war now reaching even Leonidion, the usual winter celebrations, like Saint Barbara's Day, Saint Nicholas Day and Christmas, either didn't take place that year or were observed in very subdued forms. Even my eighth birthday must have been made little of, for I remember nothing of it. I do recall New Year's Eve, though. According to Greek tradition this is a family occasion when children are allowed to stay up late and share in the adult revelry, however modestly. Mr Zouvas the Gendarmerie captain and his family joined us and we all spent the night gambling harmlessly with coins which had been made worthless by inflation. One of his daughters, a pretty girl of seventeen, won everything. Mr Zouvas, always jovial, attributed her luck to her visit to our outdoor toilet in total darkness. (Folklore held that if you stepped into excrement you'd come into money.)

Winters in that region tended to be relatively brief but could be very wet. Spells of heavy rain sent cascades down the mountainsides and the little creek in front of my uncle's house became a swollen, muddy torrent, while the river rose to the limits of its banks as it dashed seaward. Debris and anything else that chanced to be in the path of the flood was borne away on whitecaps of alarming violence. The boulders strewn over the riverbed presented immovable obstructions to the unstoppable force of the rushing waters, creating volcanic upheavals of churning water so that the whole river appeared to be boiling. On nights of hammering rain I drifted into dreams in the small room with the fireplace, my family huddled around me after evenings of talk and storytelling in which Alexandra shared her treasury of knowledge of subjects ranging from the Hundred Years War and the Franco-Prussian War to metaphysics. Listening to my sister's narratives by the dancing glow of a kerosene lamp somehow made the experience even more intimate. The wide, spacious salon, or parlor, was used only on warmer days or when we had guests. The fireplace room was where I spent most of my indoor time. There I read and read and read.

My voracious appetite for reading was noticed by the local librarian who gave me unlimited access to the library, a rarity for a child of my age. I could borrow any new book on the understanding, drummed into me, that my privileges depended on my returning all books in their original condition, a stipulation that I painstakingly honored. Since my homework rarely took me as much as half an hour I pored over my library books for hours, late into the lamplit night. I was fortunate to have Alexandra beside me to explain words beyond my comprehension.

The Leonidion winter thus unfolded into a season of adventures of mind and spirit that were to shape the rest of my boyhood and, ultimately, the man I would become.

• • •

March of 1942 covered our valley with wild spring flowers, filling the air with their scents and liberating my friends and me to resume our outdoor games and excursions into the countryside. We played after school until dusk, and on weekends just about all day. I became an expert at riding a neighbor's mule. I got to know the country-side intimately and learned to speak Tsakonika, a dialect based on the ancient Laconic language of the Spartans. A favorite pastime was climbing trees. The taller the tree, the greater the challenge. My legs and hands were always full of scratches. My Yaya, my patient grandmother, treated these wounds with time-honored remedies that she dispensed with clucks of disapproval and advice which had no effect on my unruly behavior.

Yaya was very intelligent and extremely talented. She performed miracles with a sewing machine, making all my clothes and repair-ing the ones I tore so recklessly. While the rest of us were away from the house at work or school or (in my case) play, Yaya toiled. She cleaned, she washed all our clothes, she baked. In a single day she could turn a sack of flour into many loaves of delicious brown bread, some of which she sliced and baked yet again to make hard-tack crackers. She transformed ripe red tomatoes into tomato paste or sun-dried tomatoes strung along the yard. She was a superb cook able to convert the humblest ingredients into a feast.

During those months in Leonidion it was her worn hands that held our household together.

• • •

Spring breathed fresh life into the gatherings on the plateia. One evening Nikos Mavrakis, the lawyer who kept us captivated with his eloquence, spoke of how he wished he could live to see the year

2000, when, no doubt, peace and social justice would prevail, automobiles would fly and men would build spaceships to visit the moon and planets. He voiced many other fantastic notions about what then seemed a remote future. Everyone calculated how old they'd be at the dawn of the new century and most concluded that they probably wouldn't make it. But Alexandra turned to me. "You might make it. You'll be sixty-seven years old."

• • •

I successfully finished second grade and was chosen from my class to recite some patriotic poetry at the end-of-year ceremony. The verses were about freedom from slavery. My self-esteem received a further boost when my performance was the subject of admiring comments on the plateia that evening, which may have meant more to me than the praise I received at school.

A vista of glorious days now opened up. Shirtless and barefoot, I took to the olive and almond trees in pursuit of the thousands of cicadas whose choruses serenaded the valley. We went to the sea at Lakos where the fishermen called from boat to boat with conch shells. Once I helped a group of them haul their fish-filled nets on to the beach.

But I wasn't to see the summer through in Leonidion. It was decided that the time had come for Alexandra and me to return to Kallithea.

I don't remember what explanation was given to me. Perhaps conditions at home had improved slightly and the immediate risk of starvation had receded. Whatever the reason, my sister and I went to the Gendarmerie headquarters where Mr Zouvas signed and issued our new identity cards. These were then stamped by the Italian Occupation authorities. Dr Trohanis, Leonidion's other physician, gave me a typhoid injection that made me sick for a day or two. Alexandra and I took a large wicker basket to Lakos to buy oranges, tangerines and other fruit for our family in Athens. The laden basket, which we carried for a mile or so back to Leonidion, must have weighed close to a hundred pounds and the trek exhausted us.

Alexandra fell into a fever. Her illness was more than a reaction to the exertions of our journey, however; it was a sign of an evil yet to come which no one then had any reason to suspect.

• • •

We reached the day of our departure from Leonidion with mixed feelings. We were going home to a family circle that we loved and had sorely missed. But we were saying goodbye to a place and community of which we'd become part, and which had in turn become part of us.

Our baggage was loaded on a mule and after an emotional farewell to my uncle, aunt and grandmother, Alexandra and I left our life in Leonidion behind us and set off down the tree-lined paved road to the port of Plaka. Beside us walked the muleteer and his slowly jogging beast bearing our possessions.

We were to travel all the way to Piraeus in a water taxi that was grossly overloaded with goods and people. The pure and cloudless sky was a brilliant blue as we cast off into a peaceful sea. After some hours, while skirting the eastern part of the Peloponnese in late afternoon, we became aware of a vessel approaching us at very high speed. It was first a dot on the far-off waters but it sped toward us so rapidly that it was upon us almost before we knew it. It was a gray

German torpedo boat that dwarfed our *venzina*. It drew up alongside us, only a few meters away. Its crew lined their railing, pointing automatic weapons as they scrutinized us.

The women on our craft crossed themselves, their lips moving in inaudible prayer. Our men stood still, meeting the Germans' eyes defiantly. Alexandra kept her composure, putting an arm around my shoulder with a firm squeeze as I gazed in awe at the guns trained on us, which included a small cannon manned by a helmeted sailor. It took only a few minutes for the German captain to satisfy himself that we posed no threat to the Third Reich. Their engine roared as they veered sharply and sped off, leaving us bobbing like a cork in their powerful wake. In minutes they were gone.

• • •

We resumed our voyage and as dusk approached, hours later, we put into the little port of Ermioni. Sea travel at night was strictly forbidden, besides which we needed to refuel. As we docked we found that our neighbor at anchor was none other than the torpedo boat that had intercepted us. A lone sentry stood guard with his rifle.

We all disembarked to stretch our legs in the little daylight that remained. A slight chill was in the air. Alexandra made me put on my coat and leather aviator-type hat. I pulled the fur-lined ear flaps down. As I walked past the German sentry he smiled down at me, adjusted his rifle strap on his shoulder and slipped his hands under my arms to raise me aloft, a universal gesture of adult toward child. He spoke a few words that I couldn't understand. Perhaps I reminded him of a child in his family back home in Germany. His eyes were friendly as they met mine but I felt no pleasure. He put me down and I walked away without giving him a smile or any other response.

After our walk Alexandra and I returned to our boat with the other passengers and spent the night on board, using our belongings as an improvised mattress.

• • •

We cast off at daybreak. We were at sea all day, staring hour after hour into the sunlit waters, until to the great relief of all the weary passengers we came to Piraeus, where we docked with many other little vessels in a part of the port called Lemonadika. After unloading our things we found a man with a cart who, for a pittance, helped us get them to the café where we were to meet my father as arranged by letter. Alexandra sat me at a table to watch our bags while she went to telephone him at the place where he now worked. We then waited to be reunited with this man, the beloved center of our lives, for whom we'd been separated for months.

Over an hour went by before he came into view and when at length we saw him walking toward us, my sister's mouth dropped. She whispered, perhaps to herself as much as to me, "My God! Look how old he's got!"

Our father was in his mid-forties. At the time of our departure to Leonidion he'd been consumed by worry and battered by a multitude of trials ranging from my mother's death to his arrest by the Italians, the threat of family starvation and the numerous hazards and uncertainties of the war. But he had nevertheless been vital and in his prime. The figure who now approached us, however, had aged beyond belief.

His walk, his face, his shoulders, his eyes and all the substance of his being were those of a man in his late sixties.

PART FOUR : STRANGE DREAMS

CHAPTER 18 : *LIFE AMONG THE GHOSTS*

We took the tram from Piraeus to Kallithea. On a rail trip it's normal for a child to sit glued to the window of the swaying coach as scene after scene flies by and the clickety-clack rushes one onward through an ever-changing panorama of sights. But as Alexandra and my father talked, it wasn't the world outside but he, this haggard and withered man, who held me transfixed. Aghast and in sidelong glances I absorbed his shocking new appearance as discreetly as I could.

From his once-stout frame many pounds had fallen away, which might in other circumstances have left him looking healthier. But the freshness of his skin had gone and something had been drained out of him. His whole manner betrayed the unimaginable strain under which he'd been living, or rather clinging to life. Most striking of all was that he'd lost most of his hair and what remained was gray. His persona told a story of anguish whose chapters were dismayingly added to when we arrived home. There Alexandra and I were reunited, in both tender joy and bitter sadness, with my sisters Maria and Litsa. We had left behind us two lovely girls. Now we embraced skeletons.

Because she was fluent in Italian, Maria had managed to get some work with the Greek office of Mussolini's official fascist newspaper *Il Giornale di Roma*. Their office was on Philellinon Street in Athens. A friend of my family's was of Italian descent and lived in Athens; seeing our family's desperate condition, he'd recommended her for the job. It brought in a little money at a time when employment was scarce but it came at a scalding price, for it wasn't easy for Maria to work for a newspaper that represented the enemy of Greece.

Although she was simply a young girl who sat in an office and typed with the sole aim of saving our family from starvation, going to work each day required an act of courage. This wasn't only because of Maria's internal unease with her position but also because her confused misgivings were made worse by the stinging cruelty of those in our community – not many, but enough to hurt – who accused her of collaborating with our occupiers.

Kallithea itself had changed drastically in our absence. Hunger hadn't called on our house alone. Everyone was emaciated. Alexandra was stricken with guilt because she looked so well-fed among the gaunt figures who made their weary way through the streets. A terrible and sinister sign of the darkness upon the district, and the kind of thing that a child's sharp eyes were sure to notice, was the total absence of animals. They'd either starved to death or been killed and eaten by the famished population. Butchered cats and dogs had been sold as rabbit meat or lamb. Many older people wasted away to death by sacrificing their portions of what little food there was so that younger family members would survive. Even so, the children of Kallithea, whose feet had once flown over the vacant lots, now looked like drawn and diminutive old people with legs so spindly that one wondered how they managed to stand.

Many didn't manage. Alexandra and I learned that over a two-month period in the winter of 1941-1942 the horse-drawn municipal cart had made daily rounds to collect the corpses of people who'd simply given up, lain down in some street corner, and died. This practice of picking up the dead was resumed not long after our return. From Leonidion, with its abundance of life in its lovely valley and its evenings on the plateia, I had now come to dwell in a place of ghosts.

• • •

Although Death was a wraith that made its cold touch felt only by the trail of loss it left behind it, it had minions of flesh and blood who established themselves in Kallithea in an all too visible and earthly form: the Germans.

The Reich's force in Athens had decided to disperse its military units among the population rather than massing them in large camps. This policy of embedding the units in civilian communities was aimed at making it more difficult for the Allies to strike at them from the air. To my indignation I discovered that some of my former play areas had been stolen in this way by Hitler to house his equipment. A German transport detachment had requisitioned some two and a half blocks of empty lots in our neighborhood for their trucks as well as some houses for the men. The home-owners had been paid something and evicted. Two streets were completely blocked off with barbed wire and other fortifications, and civilian residents had to make detours of a few blocks to go about their business.

One of the streets around our house, Kremou Street, was partly sealed off, with the soldiers allowing a controlled flow of local traffic. The sentries' big main gate, on Laskaridou Street, was made of wood and barbed wire and was guarded by two armed, helmeted men day and night. The military trucks that came to and from this station were dark gray with white crosses on the doors. Most of these vehicles were German-made Opel Blitzes but there were also British Bedfords that I always recognized instantly, despite their having had been painted with German colors, because the steering wheel was on the right. In their retreat the British had left these trucks behind. Along with the Blitzes they were now parked in neat rows under improvised shelters of camouflaged, corrugated tin on an open space that had been my playground.

• • •

Our new neighbors in their field-gray informs settled in as if they'd lived in Kallithea all their lives. They behaved as though they were the rightful owners of their billets, those houses at whose doorsteps and windows we'd once glimpsed friendly and familiar faces but which were now separated from us by palisades and barbed wire. I thought it peculiar that the German commanding officer had chosen to live not behind the barricades with his troops but outside with the rest of us, his enemies. Moreover, of all the houses from which he could have chosen to hang his high-peaked cap, the house he requisitioned was that of Mr and Mrs Karatzas, kitty-corner from us, where I had rung the doorbell for *podariko* on that first day of 1938. Perhaps I had brought Mr and Mrs Karatzas more good luck than they thought, for what was even odder was that the commander didn't evict Mr and Mrs Karatzas. He lived in the house with them and their servant Eleutheria, asking for no special privileges, as though he wished, fantastically, to be seen as an ordinary member of the household.

Just as my post on the terrace had given me a special vantage point from which to view the arrivals, departures and conditions of the Luftwaffe's aircraft, so fate now enabled me, through the position of our house, to watch the daily movements of this servant of Hitler. He was a tall, slender man of fifty or so, always impressively smart in his uniform, greatcoat and cap. He had a kindly, almost sad face and there was an aura of solitude about him. I never saw him with bodyguards or soldiers. He walked the short distance from the house to his barricaded compound slowly and alone, seemingly deep in thought. At the gate the guards saluted and let him in. If not for the uniform he might have been any resident of Kallithea going to work.

• • •

The changes on our streets weren't limited to the absence of the animals, the growl of the rolling German trucks, the barbed wire, the haunted and shrunken pedestrians and the sight of a Wehrmacht commander stepping pensively to the gate of his compound past silent houses where once I had played carefree with my friends. There was also the eerie vacuum left by the vanished hawkers whose operettas were no more. In their place we heard the voices of people begging in the streets for a crust of bread. These weren't beggars but ordinary folk plunged into degradation and despair. I knew some of them and their children, and in my childish breast I felt their shame. Heaviest of all within me was the crushing sense of helplessness to which all children awaken at some time or another but which is most awful when accompanied by the staggering discovery of the powerlessness of the adults whom a child has always counted on to fix all things.

An old man, so reduced to bones that it was as if someone had draped clothes over a broomstick, dragged his feet on our street and called incessantly, "I'm hungry… I'm hungry." His plea was heard continuously until he disappeared from view. A week or so later they found his body just a few streets away.

I became accustomed to the resumed and regular sight of the plodding, skinny-ribbed municipal horse whose wizened condition betokened its grisly mission as he pulled the cart of the dead around Kallithea, its driver hoisting up the corpses up like cords of wood to haul them away. My memory has turned from many of these images of the streets of my childhood, which were now like a landscape of strange dreams that turn out, when you wake up, to be horrifyingly real. But one picture is burned into my mind. There was a man everyone called Giorgo whose face was so wrinkled from starvation that at first glance you thought he was elderly and only on closer inspection could you see that he was in his early thirties. His few teeth were yellow. He was ragged and always unshaven. I believe he was mentally unbalanced, but he wasn't without survival instinct. Unlike other beggars he didn't try to evoke pity. Instead he appealed to your patriotism, urging you to invest in him all the hatred you had for the occupiers. In exchange for a morsel of food, he promised, he would wield the sword of Nemesis (in Greek mythology, the symbol of just vengeance against evil-doers) to expel the Germans from our land.

At our house Giorgo would stick his face through the bars of the little windows in our baroque front door as he rang the bell. So intense and crazed was his manner that he might indeed have been a mythological figure and the sudden appearance of his grotesque smile though the bars could have frozen the blood of even a brave and strong man who was seeing Giorgo for the first time. His voice was a croak. "Missus, you got something?" Without waiting for an answer he'd then improvise a manic ditty which would go something like, "Oh! I will kill the German bastards! For your sake, my sweet and golden dolly." After this he played an imaginary mandolin in a manner that was most disturbing to any sane observer, plucking the strings with his right hand while the fingers of his left hand danced upon the frets of the non-existent instrument with the dexterity of a virtuoso. All the while he accompanied his strumming with a demented nonsense song in his frog-like rasp: "Dringhy drin, dringhy drin, dinghy drin!"

Incredibly, all this worked very well for him. Many people gave him something, either because they got a kick out of him or just to get him out of their sight, because he clearly had no intention of ever leaving if you didn't. And perhaps he chose well in reminding our community of its ancient legend of ultimate retribution at a time when this was something they needed very much to hear, even from a madman. And the primeval powers that Giorgo claimed to represent may themselves have taken pity on him and granted him their protection, for while so many people succumbed, he somehow survived. In 1953 he would still be prowling Kallithea, offering to kill the then long-gone Germans, and assailing our neighborhood, our eardrums and our souls with his unsettling cries.

.

CHAPTER 19 : *THE TASTE OF NETTLES*

By September of 1942 the coming winter and its repercussions weighed heavily on everyone's minds. Food was likely to become even scarcer, if that were possible, and then there was the problem of clothes. Everyone wore things that were patched and frayed. Tireless labor went into altering adult garments to keep growing children warm, but cloth can be repaired and recycled only so many times and new fabric was almost unobtainable. Where blankets were cut up to make coats, this meant less cover during freezing nights. It was a fine balance in the game of survival.

I started school again and was reunited with old friends. Here too I found changes. The sheltered area in the yard that had been used for physical education or games in bad weather was now occupied by soot-covered cauldrons on improvised brick bases. In these containers bubbled a concoction of indeterminate color, taste and origin. So horrid was this substance to my eye, tongue and nose that it seemed wholly appropriate for it to swirl about in containers reminiscent of witches. It turned out that the brew was part of the Red Cross's contribution to Greece's starving children. I had to force myself to swallow the stuff, often gagging despite my hunger. The adult point of view that I now possess compels me to acknowledge that in times of war this august organization does it what it can with what it has, but my desire to be historically truthful also makes me observe that to us children, what was served up seemed appalling. Even now I wonder what was in it.

Shivering on wooden benches in our unheated school we were an utterly miserable congregation with grumbling bellies. The only difference between the classroom temperature and the frigid winter assaulting the thin walls around us was the warmth generated by our own puny bodies, and we just couldn't produce enough. Our teachers of course felt the same cold that attacked us from without and the same hunger pangs that gnawed at us within. Intelligent youngsters could plainly see that the quality of our instructors' mental focus deteriorated along with the decline in the attention spans of their pupils.

Inevitably the war intruded into our lessons, although this wasn't supposed to happen, as if not mentioning reality would protect us from it. We were now taught stirring patriotic ballads and anthems about independence, of heroes who sacrificed their lives for us, of freedom. These traditional hymns to our nation ostensibly referred to the Turkish yoke that had been imposed on us for some four centuries. But this time, by implication, they were about the Germans and the Italians as well. It was never mentioned, but the teachers, who had no other way of venting their outrage against the occupation, knew very well that this was what they were leading us in song about as our lungs expelled the icy air and our trembling voices rose to the rooftops.

We were little choirs of resistance. And we knew it.

• • •

The Allies had imposed a naval blockade on Greece to obstruct Axis shipping, but while it prevented the invaders from receiving war equipment by sea it also kept Greek civilians from receiving food through our ports. In January and February of 1943 the blockade was relaxed enough to allow the Red Cross to send in some relief supplies on ships of neutral nationality. But the amounts were small and starvation deaths continued. Many Greeks who didn't immediately perish fell prey to malnutrition-induced illnesses that eventually killed or lastingly damaged them.

The Red Cross shipments that made it through were dispatched to distribution centers for neighborhood grocers, who went there to load up their carts. People then went to the local outlets to collect their rations. In Kallithea the distribution center was Mr Rokanas' grocery store. Our neighborhood's share was then fetched by Mr Petroheilos, whose store was a block from us. To get his packed cart back to his place he had to pass by our house, which yet again seemed to have been positioned expressly to give me a front-row view of wartime events that affected our community. With much panting and puffing Mr Petroheilos pushed his cart through our street as people of all ages beheld with anticipation the mountain of sacks piled before him, all stamped with the Red Cross sign. Our mouths watered like that of a child staring at a piece of chocolate perched on a high shelf out of reach.

We went to Mr Petroheilos' store once a month, ration coupons in hand, and came away with our household's slender quota. These included Red Cross chickpeas, dried green peas and sometimes, but not often, some hazelnuts. These provisions were supplemented much later by small boxes of powdered soups which were cousins of the forbidding broth that percolated in our school cauldrons. One kind of soup we called soupa tou bakali, "grocer's soup"; the other contained diced multi-colored dried vegetables and was dubbed mosaiko, "the mosaic". I'm sure these concoctions contributed importantly to our diet but although the wise people who created them had no doubt thought carefully about their nutritional value, they'd somehow forgotten that human beings have taste buds. I had to pinch my nose while I ate.

Between our monthly visits to Mr Petroheilos' store we went daily to Mr Raptis' bakery, one of the oldest in Kallithea, where we exchanged our Red Cross coupons for a small portion of yellow bobota, something resembling corn bread. Each member of the family was entitled to one piece the size of a pack of American king-size cigarettes, which was to last us a day. I don't know what made it yellow: some said corn, cynics said sawdust. Whatever it was, it tasted to me like manna, the food that the Bible tells us God sent to the wandering Israelites. I loved it. It was baked in large pans on wax paper and it was impossible to separate the bobota entirely from the wax paper, but I ate it paper and all so I wouldn't lose a single crumb. Many times my father gave me his portion.

• • •

Hunger was our constant companion. I went to bed with an unfilled stomach; I awoke with an even emptier one. Certain foods receded from my sense of reality so much that their names and images seemed to be figments of my imagination rather than memories of what we'd actually eaten in the past. Sometimes not even a most intense reverie could bring them back to mind all their nuances of flavor. I could remember the whiteness of sugar, which was now as rare as snow in the Sahara, but I often found myself struggling to recall its taste. I readily recreated it on my tongue only on the very rare occasions when my father brought home haroupomelo, a honeylike extract from carobs. One spoonful of this was enough to bring about ecstasy.

The smell and taste of meat similarly evaporated from my imagination. As for coffee, the grand days on Leonidion's plateia now seemed like episodes from a storybook, for coffee was gone from our lives. Some people roasted and ground up rye to make a coffee substitute, a practice that made them seem particularly rich not only because they had this beverage to enjoy but because if our family had possessed any rye we'd have made bread with it. And the simple pleasures of a chocolate or a piece of candy became as remote from our lives as the age of the dinosaurs. The kiosk at the square called Perivolaki, Little Orchard, from which I'd stolen a chocolate, incurring my mother's wrath, was now run by Militsa, the owner's daughter. The only candy she had to sell was made with substitute ingredients including soapwort herbs. Few could afford to buy even ersatz candy now and if they did, it didn't taste like the candy they knew; it left a bitterness in the mouth.

Although I should have been grateful for being kept alive, I felt rage at what we didn't have, and at the food that once we'd known and which now, for reasons I couldn't fully grasp, was no more.

• • •

But while children can feel a towering anger and indignation, survival instincts also make them capable of prodigious feats of stoicism that adults often underestimate once their own childhoods are far enough behind them. I soon came to understand that hunger was a part of my daily routine that I just had to accept. I was told how much worse it had been in my neighborhood during my time away in Leonidion and I'm still thankful to have been spared those even more dreadful earlier scenes of people being cut down unmercifully, and in nightmarish numbers, in the streets of my Kallithea as weakness from hunger, and death from famine, overtook them.

I received other instructive comparisons, too, to help me nourish my sense of proportion, resilience and ability to adapt. A refugee boy from Russia, whose family had been expelled from their land by Stalin and had known dire hunger even before the war, taught me how to still my restless cravings by eating nettles. On our way to school we went into empty fields and picked as many as time allowed, carefully using twigs to keep our fingers from the stingers as we peeled them and ate the stems. They tasted like lettuce. Although they did very little to quell my appetite this harvesting became a routine of my walks to school, perhaps because there was a psychological comfort just in being able to go through the motions of eating something more or less at will. The carob trees growing here or there, on which donkeys had munched before the war, became another target. My missions to the bakery took me past the Athanasoulias family's house, and I'd stop to climb the carob tree there and pick some pods to chew on. Their pulp and seeds had an astringent taste but kept me going for a spell.

• • •

It wasn't just that all commodities were scarce but that there was hardly any meaningful way of obtaining what little was still available. Hyperinflation subjected the Greek currency, the drachma, to a catastrophic devaluation as the war proceeded, making money worthless as a means of exchange until the post-war authorities implemented a vast currency adjustment. In his civilian job before being called into uniform for his post at The Barracks, my father had been an accountant at the Greek branch of a British insurance company, Licenses & General, on Hippokratous Street in Athens. His salary was modest but afforded us a comfortable living, enough to put us in the middle-class bracket. With the German Occupation the British connection was severed and the insurance office in Athens became associated with a French company, La Fonciere. Paying for insurance would have been a low priority for most Greeks at that time, so the office may have functioned purely as an administration facility for people with existing policies. I don't know what my father earned but it couldn't have been much, because what he made in a month bought us about twelve pounds of bread or its price equivalent in whatever else was available. Because of the hyperinflation, even ordinary things had outlandish prices. One loaf of bread cost around a hundred and fifty million drachmas. Later the highest denomination people used in their transactions was a ten-billion-drachma banknote.

The value of money changed so quickly that my father's salary began to lose whatever value it had the moment it was paid to him. Within a few weeks his payday currency, like the tiny sums brought in by Maria's typing at the newspaper and like the cash income of all other Greek workers, was given to us children to play with. It was worthless for buying anything in the real world. In practice the only way to "buy" anything was by barter. But my father had long since sold everything in our house that we could afford to part with.

• • •

One of the hardest things we had to accept was learning to live without olive oil. We got no oil or fat from the Red Cross or anyone else. Anyone who knows anything at all about Greeks will know that this was an extraordinary adjustment. From a diet that virtually centered on foods prepared in olive oil we now ate only food boiled in water. The most readily available food was lachanides or collard greens, leafy vegetables that gave us Vitamin C and fiber but, when cooked without oil, few calories to energize our faltering bodies. After the war the word lachanides lived on in the vocabulary of Greeks as a synonym for deprivation.

And so the innocent and universal question in any household -- "What's for dinner today? -- was now moot. Every morning we already knew the answer. Either it would be whatever our father managed to scrounge that day, with fresh ingenuity or by thinking of some new sacrifice, or come dinner time there'd be somber silence and a tender embrace, with my elders holding me close so I couldn't see the bitten lips that held back those most rending tears of all, which are shed when one has done all one can, trying with everything the exhausted human body and will and spirit can possibly muster, and still it hasn't been enough.

German soldiers pass through a Greek village.

CHAPTER 20 : ROCKET TO THE MOON

The pitch-black winter nights of the war were an experience that's difficult for most people to imagine today, when even in the darkest rural areas some diffused light always pervades the atmosphere, if only from cities many miles away. Back then, in the absolute and wide-ranging blackout, starless and cloudy winter nights enveloped us in depths so inky we might have been in a sealed vault in the bowels of the earth. Walking outside you had to move slowly, as if blind, staying on the sidewalk, your fingertips feeling the wall to grope your way, and sometimes bumping into others coming from the opposite direction. An advantage of this utter darkness was that on starry nights no human source intruded on the brilliance of the jewels strewn across the sky. My father pointed out the constellations to me and taught me to find Polaris, the North Star.

The stark blackness enshrouded us with a biting cold that was relentless. My elders said this winter of 1942-1943 was one of the worst they could remember. The air in our house was glacial. We slept fully clothed under as many blankets as we had. Every morning we scraped ice off the inside of the window panes before we could look out at the new day.

Once a week a big Italian truck arrived at the German compound heaped with sacks of coal for heating. How we envied them! Whenever I saw the truck I made a quick dash for it. While the Italians unloaded the sacks they always left the engine running and I stood behind the exhaust to keep warm, ignoring the soot that blackened my legs, for it bathed me in a warmth I hadn't felt at home or school for months, and I treasured it. As a bonus, a few pieces of coal sometimes fell out of the overflowing bags. These I carefully collected and took home for our cooking. I sorely wished I could take away enough to warm our house.

At least one member of our family was ill and bedridden at any time because the famine and lack of vitamins had undermined our health. We developed boils all over our bodies. Since we had no medicine, not even rubbing alcohol for disinfecting, the only cure was to wait for them to ripen, squeeze the pus out and wipe them with a clean wet cloth. Perhaps this helped spread the infection because when one boil healed another started.

We all suffered from chilblains, our fingers and toes swelling into purple sausages that not only hurt but itched excruciatingly and oozed a whitish liquid. There was no cure but heat. Some people swore that the best treatment was to urinate on the affected parts. We couldn't bring ourselves to try it.

• • •

In Leonidion the huddling of the family around the fireplace had promoted talk and storytelling, which, along with my avid reading, gave wings to my fertile imagination. Something similar now happened in Kallithea. In the evenings we all gathered in our dining room, closed the door to contain heat and sat around the table conversing, spinning anecdotes or reading. Eventually the warmth of our bodies raised the room temperature slightly to make it more bearable. Sometimes we curled our fingers around hot cups of weak tea which was fortified on luckier nights with a dash of Metaxa brandy. Retreated thus in the fragile sanctuary of our home, assailed by war, cold and hunger, we were sustained by inner resources of the spirit. When the body is besieged the mind offers refuge and we spent hours reading. We read to escape, to gain mental compensation, and to help us look to a better future, however distant.

My father's extensive library, centered on the collection of leather-bound books in our big walnut cabinet (all in Greek, of course), contained a treasury of world literature and wisdom. I read in our dining room or bundled up in bed. We voraciously devoured these volumes, public library books and reading matter borrowed from neighbors. Anything would do, from pulp detective story magazines to classic literature. After reading *The Invisible Man*, by H.G. Wells, I took pleasure in explaining to my family that the *Invisible Man* would have been blind since if light passed unimpeded through the eye, as it would in a transparent person, vision couldn't work. I think only Alexandra understood. I read a French story, perhaps influenced by Jules Verne's *From the Earth to the Moon* or Wells' *First Men in the Moon*, in which a scientist made a moon rocket. I excitedly designed my own version. At the Etoile cinema a vendor of roasted pumpkin seeds sold me (for a few million drachmas) some lamp carbide. I joined three empty cans together, fashioned a paper nose cone and built a launchpad of mud and stones in the vacant lot behind our house. With a bang and a whoosh my rocket went straight into our neighbor Miss Poppy's open window, muddying her white curtains. She screamed and I hid for days until her wrath abated. But I was far from alone in my missile interests: at that same time Germany scientists were creating the V-2 rockets that would later target London.

• • •

While my reading and my imagination distracted me from my hunger, others took more active paths to cope with the famine. These included the *saltadoroi* (jumpers) and the *mavragotites* (black marketeers).

The *saltadoroi* were daring, ingenious thieves who stole food from the Occupation forces at great risk to their lives. Our neighbor Mr Hadjimihalis told us of a German truckload of food parked on the street under an armed sentry's watchful eyes. Three *saltadoroi* studied the situation and devised a strategy. Two slipped behind the truck while their associate, an unlit cigarette dangling from his lips, approached from the front and greeted the sentry politely. He stooped to press the unlit cigarette on one of the truck's headlights, inhaling furiously. Incredulous, the soldier watched the spectacle of an apparent imbecile trying to light a cigarette on the cold glass cover of an electric light. While he was thus distracted, laughing at this hilarious display of what he took to be the stupidity of Greeks, his entertainer's two compatriots nimbly and soundlessly climbed into the back of the truck and lightened its load by a couple of boxes of food with which they quickly departed. The jumpers were well-named, for they had to move like lightning. They also had to have nerves of steel. A German bullet awaited those who stumbled or dallied a second too long.

The *mavragotites*, black marketeers, were of two sorts. In one group were heartless schemers who took callous advantage of wartime scarcity and suffering to enrich themselves, like food hoarders who sold at exorbitant prices when their customers were desperate. A common expression of the time, "Aganda, Rommel!", signified the dim view that most Greeks took of such profiteers. To Greek sailors handling ropes on a boat, aganda means "hold on, steady". The story behind "Aganda, Rommel!" was that as long as the Allied naval blockade was in force, black marketeers would go on exploiting the starving. It was believed that the blockade would be lifted only when the war turned against the German troops in North Africa, headed by Rommel. The Red Cross could then start bringing us supplies and the black marketeers would be out of business. The slogan "Hold on, Rommel!" was thus contemptuously cited as a prayer uttered by black marketeers who hoped Rommel would dig in as long as possible. The phrase became a derogatory Greek term for greedy people in general.

The second kind of black marketeers consisted of poor, ordinary Greeks who simply used their entrepreneurial skills to trade in hard-to-get commodities. While their prices may have reflected the trouble to which they'd gone to procure their wares, they weren't all callous extortionists. Some black marketeers went deep into the countryside for the produce they bartered in neighborhoods like Kallithea, walking up to fifty miles to acquire their produce. And since conventional transportation was now extremely limited, enterprising black marketeers fashioned carts with wheels from bicycles, baby carriages and just about anything else. Most prized of all were the runner wheels from the tracks of destroyed British tanks. These not only had rubber treads but roller bearings too, which made the carts easier to push.

To obtain something on the black market therefore didn't always or necessarily mean you were dealing with bloodsuckers. A fair barter was possible, assuming you had something that the other party wanted.

• • •

We now had school only half a day and sometimes not at all. I had plenty of time for games with my friends in the streets. Despite all the monstrous things happening around us we were, after all, still children. We even played at war, with stones flying this way and that. You'd think we'd have had enough of war, but my curiosity about the trappings of war and soldiers remained as strong as ever and I was inevitably drawn to investigate the Wehrmacht compound in our neighborhood. There I not only met German soldiers but, with the openness that comes naturally to children, I innocently struck up a friendship with a couple.

Arthur was in his twenties, tall, blond and always smiling. Alfred was in his thirties, avuncular and kind. They lived on the corner in Mr Kyriakopoulos' two-story house. Sometimes they came out of the barbed-wire enclosure and we played football in the adjacent empty field with a ball I'd made of rags. When I scored I shouted "Gholl !", the Greek pronunciation of "goal". When they scored they'd shout, "Tor!", the same in German. Despite the language barrier we understood one another. Since they let me win most of the time, I started shouting, "Tor!" myself whenever I scored, out of courtesy.

When Arthur and Alfred were around I walked into the German enclosure without fear. I often sat on the steps with them and other soldiers listening to them laugh and talk in German without any idea of what they were talking or laughing about. Despite our friendship, they never gave me anything to eat. Someone told me their rules forbade it and that they had a sign in their camp saying, *"German soldiers: Do not feed Greek children because when they grow up they will fight you."*

• • •

Winter receded. As everyone looked forward to the spring and summer of 1943 there was a positive effect on people's outlooks and behavior. Chairs appeared on the sidewalks again and neighbors sat on their steps to gossip. Greetings were exchanged in our street as familiar faces passed, albeit aged by hardship and in numbers thinned by the deaths in our community. It was reassuring to have evidence that the seasons continued to turn on time-honored hinges, like never-changing scenes from a beloved old movie. As the icy days left us we needed fewer calories and began to feel better despite our paltry rations. And we could again start growing a few vegetables on the terrace to supplement the basic foodstuffs we received from the Red Cross. It was especially heartening when wild flowers returned to the empty lots. They too had triumphed over another winter.

To our vast joy, stray cats started returning. They were presumably descendants of the enterprising felines that had escaped becoming someone's dinner during the worst of the famine. These prowling beasts were now welcomed by one and all with a gladness that surely hadn't greeted cats since the days of ancient Egypt. With the haughtiness of their kind they adopted households all around the neighborhood and we too, acquired one. Fortunately she didn't demand food from us because she was a huntress and could see to herself. She needed only shelter and affection, which we were happy to give. Not only did she become part of our family but she presented us with kittens every spring for years.

My roamings around Kallithea were now wholly on bare feet because I'd outgrown my shoes. Leather being unavailable, canvas shoes with twisted rope soles had become common. I had such a pair but they were for evenings only. For a little more money one could buy sandals with rubber soles recycled from discarded automobile tires but these were hard to find and in any case we couldn't afford them.

The important thing was that the grim winter was over and we were, it seemed, surviving after all, and it didn't matter that I had no shoes; it mattered only that there was sun again and warmth and that I could go out and run and feel the sidewalk and the grass beneath my toes. Eleni Velmahou, the piano teacher, began practicing her repertoire for her year's teaching schedule, as she always did when spring and summer came. Her playing could be heard three blocks down the street. On the steps of Mr Kyriakopoulos' house German soldiers sat quiet and rapt as music crashed and wafted upon and over and through us all. The notes of Brahms, Beethoven and Chopin flowed in the air like plumes of glory that made you want to laugh and sing and cry at the sheer wonder of being alive.

When I look back at that time, what is most meaningful in my memory is not the events so much as the people. Most of them have gone into the years now, yet are still as fresh before my mind's eye as they were in 1943. Eleni, the piano teacher whose music heralded the spring of that year, lived with her widowed mother in a rambling house on the corner of our street and Kremou Street. With them dwelt other widows whose husbands had fallen in the war. It was a house of mourning, of figures in black.

Eleni had a sister and a brother, Aris, who appeared to be quite ordinary and unassuming. We would later discover that he'd been a member of a Greek Resistance organization, the Greek People's Liberation Army, or ELAS. Some of the neighborhood teenagers and young men used to gather on the front steps of the Lithorikis house. One of them, Mimis Christodoulou, was a multi-talented boy of eighteen who never refused a request to make me a toy. He played his guitar on the steps as he and his friends sang the popular songs of the day. Mimis was killed not too long afterwards when Greek turned against Greek in a civil war. But the chords of his guitar as he strummed on those steps, and the images of his agile fingers making me some simple plaything, and the voices of his companions, are with me still.

As the teenage boys assembled, so the girls, too, paraded, hoping to catch the eye of a favored young man. All the while the German soldiers sat on the steps of their billets taking in the evening air, smoking, talking quietly among themselves, or just silently watching the young men and girls re-live the courtship rituals of the ages.

My Father had this Luger ...

When the curfew was extended to midnight the socializing extended to the Palladion, the open-air movie theater a block from our house. Until it grew dark enough to begin the movies they advertised the show by playing music from loudspeakers that could be heard for blocks. When the movie began, things quietened down again. Sitting on their front steps or on chairs on the sidewalk, people made small talk that for a while gave life a semblance of normality. They gossiped, reminisced, exchanged jokes. They didn't talk about the war.

I sat on our front steps, lost in my own dreams when the talk bored me. But I found much entertainment in the stories that our neighbors told one another to divert themselves from their anxieties, like Mr Hadjimihalis' tale of his childhood in 1910, when Halley's Comet had made one of its periodic visits. Some people, he related, had feared that the comet would collide with our planet. Members of his own family and some of their neighbors believed doomsday was imminent and decided to enjoy their last moments in a big party that lasted into the small hours. Afterwards, while everyone was asleep, a cat bumped into a large pot-plant and it fell from a balcony with a crash. The noise wrenched everybody awake and they all jumped up and stumbled around in panic, convinced that the end of the world had come. With anecdotes like these my elders raised enough laughter to keep the threat of wartime doom at bay, the way a child arms itself against the darkness by whistling past a cemetery or a supposedly haunted house.

• • •

A few minutes before the midnight curfew the chairs were taken indoors and the shutters were closed to observe the blackout while the lights were turned on for a while. At length they were extinguished and the shutters reopened to admit the spring breeze into the dark houses, and we all slept if hunger would permit it.

While the shutters were still closed and the lights were on, however, my family had its own activity in our house, and it was both exciting and frightening, not least because it was a matter of the utmost secrecy. And here I must explain a remarkable thing. It's strange to write of our invaders, the Germans who'd occupied our country and my neighborhood, that they didn't bother us. But they didn't. They kept to themselves. Other than commandeering the houses and spaces they used to house their men and equipment, and of course being part of the conditions of war that had caused our famine, they didn't interfere directly with the everyday lives of the people of Kallithea. Indeed, having a detachment of the German Army as neighbors was an advantage for us in the evening activities behind closed doors and shutters that I'll now describe, because the German presence afforded us a degree of protection from the Gestapo, Hitler's dreaded secret police. After all, what Greek would be so rash as to engage in a subversive act under the very noses of an entire Wehrmacht compound?

But the Gestapo hadn't met my father. He not only flouted the Germans' strict radio censorship law by daring to listen to BBC Radio every night, but he compounded this serious offense by allowing a group of eager neighbors into our home to join him in this forbidden act.

All this took place with a horde of Germans camped on our doorstep and with a long, conspicuous radio antenna stretched along our the terrace to advertise our crime against the Reich.

• • •

{ 187 }

It was thanks to the BBC's Greek-language service that the temperature in our house rose slightly in the evenings, for when our *Er-Ce-Ah* beamed its dose of hope to us every evening the population of our home increased. My father's friends who came nightly to share the latest news from London knew very well, as he did, that adults found listening to foreign broadcasts could be arrested and sent to a concentration camp, or summarily shot. But because of my father's decision to disobey the Germans and keep our *Er-Ce-Ah* unfettered by the tampering of the Occupation censors, we now possessed our neighborhood's only radio that could receive BBC broadcasts, and there was a desperate hunger for reliable news. Our house thus became a clandestine news center for the receipt of bulletins from London.

Our dining room was the subject of careful theatrical staging to support this illegal and enormously hazardous activity. A deck of cards was cunningly placed on the table beside a handful of chickpeas. The idea was that if we were raided by the Gestapo the radio would hastily be turned off and the adults would sit around the table pretending to be playing cards and using the chickpeas as gambling chips. On the wall was a big school map of Europe, and even though the borders of the countries no longer reflected wartime realities it was good enough to enable everybody to follow the BBC reports. No one was allowed to mark the map in any way to make the radio announcements more intelligible. Thus, if the Gestapo came it could be claimed that the map was used for school geography studies.

The routine was always the same. Nikos Malatestas, our next door neighbor, came first. After him came Nikos Hadjimihalis, who lived across from our house. Then, one by one, the Syrakos brothers, Ilias, Hippocrates and Nikos.

They didn't ring the bell. One of us waited at the door and the moment we heard a small, discreet tap, we let them in. Once inside they took their seats, speaking in low voices, to await the broadcast while I or one of my sisters stood guard at the front door. If any footstep approached the house a prearranged warning silenced the radio at once and the group around the table transformed themselves into a group of friends innocently playing cards as if they'd been doing so all evening.

$$\bullet\ \bullet\ \bullet$$

While they listened intently to a BBC broadcast these ordinary men of my community were transformed. They conducted themselves exactly like a conference of generals and our dining room took on the atmosphere of a war room of top military planners. The group sagely deliberated on the latest developments in the war, astutely eyeing the map on the wall to trace troop movements and the locations of battles. My father had a fine presence and a leader's demeanor, and his record of military experience, culminating in his governance of The Barracks, had given him an air of command. He looked every inch like a supremo presiding over generals who in turn directed the armies of a great power. I say this not only from the impressions formed by a child's eyes but also from the more educated perspective that I later developed as an adult after reading much history and watching many documentaries and other films. My father's friends in turn carried themselves at these sessions with an earnestness befitting any high officer of weighty responsibilities. Neither Churchill nor Eisenhower nor Hitler not Caesar himself could have had a more qualified-looking group of strategic advisors than these Greeks of my neighborhood gathered around our dining room table with its chickpeas. Anyone observing them and eavesdropping on them with no knowledge of their identities would have taken them for a vital cadre of leaders responsible for decisions of critical importance to the outcome of the war and the fates of nations.

• • •

My father was always in charge of the radio. The most dangerous part of these evenings of secret contact with London was tuning our *Er-Ce-Ah* to the prohibited frequency. In the shortwave band the radio whistled and snorted and crackled uncertainly until my father found the station. Those sharp, penetrating sounds were easily audible even when the volume was turned down low, so everyone held their breaths as my father's fingers sensitively twisted the dial this way and that in search of the right place, like a safecracker seeking the exact combination. A sudden burst of piercing noise could carry far and give us away to an educated German ear that recognized the radio's shriek for what it was. The tautness in the air was relieved only when the BBC signature was finally heard: the first notes of Beethoven's Fifth Symphony, da-da-da DAHH, which also evoke three dots and a dash in Morse code, signifying the letter V for Victory. This introduction was sometimes preceded by the chimes of Big Ben, the bell of the clock tower at London's Westminster Palace. Then a voice said: *"Edo Lonthinon."* ("This is London.")

And everyone would cluster around the radio, heads almost touching.

The faces of the listeners mirrored what the BBC told us. A triumph against the Axis brought smiles and made heads nod in satisfaction; a grim report resulted in creased foreheads and tightened lips; a neutral broadcast, relating nothing worse than usual nor anything particularly good, was met just by sober concentration as every listener strained to catch every word lest some crucial item be missed.

When the transmission ended my father and his friends stood before the map on the wall to discuss what they'd heard and exchange opinions on its implications. Over the many months in which they used our *Er-Ce-Ah* to follow the progress of the war through its phases, they not only mastered the geography of various fronts in detail but became acquainted with commanders by name.

"Things are really bad for the Germans in Stalingrad. I don't think they're going to last."

"Rokossovsky will cook Paulus' goose."

Hippocrates, the intellectual of the group, tended to be more specific. "Their best move is to head for Voronezh and Kursk even before they take Stalingrad. This way they will trap those in the Crimea."

Every view prompted another. "Why not head for the Sea of Azov and do it from there?"

When they exhausted one area of debate they found another. The doings of Rommel in North Africa could also be counted on for lively conversation.

"Rommel is finished in North Africa. The Germans in Tunisia are on their last legs."

"I think they'll now start their invasion from Greece."

"No, they'll go for Sicily. It's closer to Tunisia."

• • •

Of all these men my father had the most field experience. Military service was obligatory for all able-bodied men when they reached twenty-one, and all those who came to our BBC evenings had been in uniform. But my father had served longer than any and outranked them all, so his opinions carried weight. But the playing field was level when the talk turned from the military aspects of the war to its politicians. Every Greek man considers himself an expert at politics. "I don't trust Stalin," an older and more bourgeois neighbor would say.

"I don't trust Churchill," Hippocrates would counter.

An amusing feature of these evenings was that when anyone prefaced a comment with the name "Niko" there was momentary confusion because three of the dining room generals had the same name.

The discussions were supposed to be conducted in subdued voices, but on at least two occasions my father and his friends got so carried away that they shouted, putting us all at peril from the Germans nearby. Once was when Hitler's forces surrendered at Stalingrad; the other was when the Allies landed in Sicily. Both events caused happy whoops, igniting the optimism that is so intrinsic to the Greek character.

But their glad outbursts turned out to be somewhat premature.

Archbishop Damaskinos.

CHAPTER 22 : *PEOPLE LIKE MOSES*

While the BBC was our most trusted news source, it wasn't the only one. There were, of course, the newspapers controlled by the occupying forces, like the Italian one where my sister Maria worked. And then there was Mr Karatzas' maid, Eleutheria.

In pre-war times many middle-class Greek households employed maids who lived on the premises, usually a village girl from a poor family. A maid often came to be regarded as a member of her employers' family, living with them for years until she married. Maids who remained unmarried could become lifelong fixtures in a house, even outliving their employers. The relationship wasn't always comfortable as there were employers who mistreated their maids. But anyone trying this on Eleutheria would have met their match.

She was in her late twenties and had been with the Karatzas family as long as I could remember. She was formidably independent and stood her ground against all comers. Not only could she whittle anyone down to size with her razor-sharp tongue but she seemed to know everything that was happening in our community. Her astonishing fund of constantly updated intelligence about everyone's business wasn't only entertaining but a genuine source of endlessly fascinating news. Eleutheria had truly missed her calling, for it was easy to imagine her as an investigative reporter for a great newspaper or a news agency like Reuters, tracking down the intimate details of her fellow citizens' lives with the infallible instincts of a bloodhound. As with the best and most determined journalists, it was vital to her to be the first to tell you the news. She shared her findings generously, indeed insistently, with the skill of a gifted raconteur.

On meeting any of my elders in the street she grabbed them by the sleeve to divulge the latest tidbit, looking them straight in the eyes so as to savor their reaction to her new revelation.

It was the German commander's misfortune that of all the houses he could have chosen for his billet, he happened upon the one in which Eleutheria lived and worked. He might as well have taken up residence in a houseful of British and American spies. There was little about this taciturn officer's personal habits and routine that we didn't find out from Eleutheria. We could have compiled a respectable file on his personality and habits. We knew he was extremely polite and fastidiously clean, that he shared his food with the elderly Karatzas couple and that he always gave them first claim on the bathroom. We learned from our unimpeachable source that he was left-handed, that he had long, manicured fingers, and that he listened to classical music on his phonograph until late at night. The only reason we didn't yet know the color of his underwear was that his laundry was done at his compound.

One day Eleutheria came by while some of the dining room generals were in our home, and she announced, beaming, that she had a new funny story, and it was about the Jews. Through whatever mysterious means she used to obtain her information, she had learned that a family we knew, living just two blocks from the German camp, had taken in some Jews. "They told their grandmother that the newcomers were distant cousins from a town in northern Greece and the poor grandmother swallowed it!"

Not only that, she continued, laughing, "but some priest issued them Orthodox baptism certificates and they now go to church every Sunday with the family, cross themselves and kiss the icons like the others, pretending to be Christians."

She was ready to provide more details but one of the generals interrupted her and told her sternly to keep her mouth shut if she didn't want to be responsible for getting the Jews and their protectors shot. The rest shook their heads in somber agreement.

The generals had good reason for consternation, for they and my father knew something that my sisters and I were not to be told until after the German withdrawal from Greece. Next door, on the ground floor of the home of one of the dining room generals, Mr Nikos Malatestas, lived the elderly Mr Magnis with his wife Ortence and their daughter Vivi. A few months earlier they'd acquired a "tenant", a courteous young man they called Angelos Konstantinidis, who kept to himself. We would later be told that that had not been his real name and that he was, in fact, a son of a prominent Jewish family, the founders of one of the largest pasta manufacturing firms in Greece. The Magnis family had risked their lives to shelter him under their roof across the street from a German compound.

• • •

When I first heard of the Jews they were known to me only through references that I'd heard in church to people like Moses and other personages from the Bible. I hadn't realized that we had Jewish fellow citizens in the present day, as Greek as my own family, who were at even greater danger from the invaders than we were. It wasn't Eleutheria who introduced me to this fact, but our neighbor Hippocrates, one of the three Syrakos brothers who made up my father's war cabinet of dining room generals. Hippocrates told us one day that the Germans were rounding up all the Jews in Greece to send them to concentration camps in Germany and that he'd managed to hide some of these cruelly persecuted Greeks with Christian Greek families. I had to ask Alexandra to explain to me who the Jews were.

The ploy of protecting Jews by disguising them as Christians wasn't unique to the family about whom Eleutheria had told us. Archbishop Damaskinos, the head of the Greek Orthodox Church who was to serve briefly as Prime Minister of Greece at the end of the war, secretly wrote to his priests during the round-up of Greek Jews, telling them to issue Christian baptismal certificates to Jews to save them from arrest. With the cooperation of the police and local authorities, officials opened a false archive to enter the names of the Jewish citizens as Christians. The Archbishop also asked monasteries to hide as many Jewish families as possible, and he wrote to the local German commander protesting the persecution. When the commander threatened him with execution, Damaskinos' replied: "According to the traditions of the Greek Orthodox Church, our prelates are hanged, not shot. Please respect our traditions!" The nonplussed commander backed down.

Hearing about the Jews was an important step in my education. It made me aware that there were Greeks of whom I knew little or nothing. It also exposed me for the first time to the fact that people not only went to war for reasons I couldn't understand but that, even more bewilderingly, they singled out certain groups for special victimization. It was also the beginning of my first youthful insight into the murkiness of the lines between right and wrong, for here was the spiritual leader of Christian Greece protecting the innocent by asking his own people to tell lies.

I was growing up.

• • •

A new development now occurred in the saga of our *Er-Ce-Ah*. In an attempt to clamp down even more tightly on our access to information which might boost our morale and help the Greek Resistance, Mussolini announced in June of 1943 that the use of radio antennae on houses in Greece was forbidden. That very evening the dining room generals held an extraordinary council to discuss the Duce's edict. My father wished to ignore it and his neighbors unanimously agreed. Mussolini was far away and the Germans, who were so close, seemed to care not a hoot. So our faithful *Er-Ce-Ah* was allowed for a while to continue pricking up its ears and relaying the BBC's bulletins to us, regardless of the heightened threat.

Soon, however, things took an even more disturbing turn. Unknown faces began appearing in the neighborhood. In our small community everyone knew almost everybody else. Given the watchful circumstances of the Occupation, any stranger immediately drew attention and aroused suspicion. When my father and his friends realized that strangers were being spotted on our streets, they took this very seriously. The dining room generals concluded that Gestapo agents were looking the area over. There was considerable unease. Even if we weren't caught listening to the BBC, our mere possession of an uncensored radio could have the gravest consequences. It was too late to take it to the authorities to have it sealed against foreign broadcasts since the deadline was long past. A possible solution was to destroy our *Er-Ce-Ah*, but no one wanted that, for who knew when this latest danger would recede?

After much discussion a plan was devised. Up to then we'd relied on our proximity to the Wehrmacht to camouflage our radio use against the prying eyes of the Gestapo. Now the time had come to move the *Er-Ce-Ah* itself to a new home that the Gestapo would never suspect. In a fresh irony, we sought to receive unwitting protection from our other foes, the Italians. It was resolved that the safest place to store our radio was none other than the Athens office of the Italian newspaper Il Giornale di Roma, where my sister Maria worked. She approached her boss, Colonel Cesarini, took the considerable risk of telling him the truth, and asked him if we could bring the radio there. Fortunately her intuitions about his political sympathies were right: like many of his compatriots, he was a reluctant ally of the Germans, and he agreed to take the radio in. So our *Er-Ce-Ah* was unceremoniously wrapped in a blanket and Maria, helped by a friend, took it by tram to her office. It was a tense journey because this was a time of active subversion by the Resistance and increasing surveillance by the Gestapo. My sister and her companion might have been stopped at any point by an official demanding to know exactly what was in that bulky bundle. It was their very good luck that no one did.

• • •

The loss of our *Er-Ce-Ah* left a hole in our dining room and in our lives. We were bereft of not just a piece of furniture nor even a source of music but a lifeline of hope, our connection with that London on whose voice our liberation depended. The radio was like a member of our household. For years it had been part of our family life through illness, celebration, laughter and the shedding of many tears including those of death. As for the dining room generals, they were now mariners without a ship. It is a sign of what those evenings around our table had come to mean to all of them that they went on meeting in our home nightly, just as before, despite the absence of the device that had formed the center of their assemblies. They still discussed the war but it wasn't the same. They now had not the BBC's bulletins to use as their guiding star but only their own unaided speculations as to what might be happening out on the battlefields of Europe and the other far-flung theaters of the war. Moreover, the removal of the hazard of discovery by the Gestapo was a coin with two faces. It was an undeniable relief that a burden of such immense risk had been lifted from shoulders of my father and his friends. On the other hand, the conspiratorial nature of those evenings gathered around the radio, and the peril of discovery hanging over them like a sword poised to fall at any moment, had somehow made them soldiers. In listening to that radio they had defied and, in a sense, taken on the enemy, and that made them one with the Resistance. Now they were only a group of men sitting around a dining room table.

Still, I would always remember them as generals.

• • •

My elders' fears of German crackdowns were amply justified. One night in August the tram depot in Kallithea burned down with ninety-three trams in it. The Germans accused the depot staff of sabotage, since while damaging the transport system hurt Greeks it also hurt the German effort to conduct the Occupation in a manner that suited them. They started rounding people up and announced that they were going to execute a hundred or so, including some of our neighbors. Archbishop Damaskinos intervened and the Germans let their suspects go. But with fewer trams, the lines of people who needed to take a tram to work stretched around the plateia. Maria was one of those workers, for she still took a tram into Athens to work at the newspaper, although those days were drawing to an end. One day she returned from work with an announcement. The war had been going against Italy; both its military machine and its government were teetering on the brink of collapse. Consequently, the Athens office of Il Giornale di Roma was to close.

The paper's head, Colonel Cesarini, gathered all the employees to tell them this would be their last week. After sharing this news he took my sister aside and told her she should take our radio home, otherwise when the Germans took the office over they would confiscate it. A family council was held, this time excluding the generals, and it was decided that our radio should be rescued and restored to our home where it belonged.

Once again Maria, accompanied by a neighbor, went to the newspaper office and once more our *Er-Ce-Ah* was wrapped in a blanket. Once more they bore him to a tram and once more they managed to make the tense trip home without being accosted by a prying official. There was great glee when they entered our house with the bundle. Gratefully and even lovingly we unwrapped our bringer of music and prohibited nightly access to the latest chapters in the war provided by the trusted, inspiring voice of London. Risk or no risk, it made our hearts feel indescribably good to see that cumbersome instrument back in its place in our dining room.

This was no mere machine. A dear old friend had come home.

CHAPTER 23 : *IMAGES ON A SCREEN*

It's difficult to separate the larger historic events of the war from the story of my family life with distinct boundaries. They were interwoven like threads in a single cloth. The closure of the Italian newspaper office marked the end of a cycle of personal development for my sister Maria. Her employment wasn't only significant for our sustenance; it also defined an important phase of her emergence as a young woman. As for me, I was one of countless Greeks whom the war robbed, in a way, of much that is normal in childhood, exposing us to things no child should experience. Of course we still grew up, those of us who were lucky enough to survive, and we still went through many of the usual rites of passage, but our view of the world and of ourselves was unquestionably different from those of children who grow up in peacetime. For better or worse the war produced a generation that learned to take on responsibilities prematurely.

With my father's attention consumed by the stresses of wartime privation, risk and survival, my sisters cared for me in a way that bordered on the parental. During her time at the newspaper Maria often took me with her to the newspaper office where I remained until we rode the tram home again together. She had to ask her boss, Colonel Cesarini, for permission to bring her little brother to the office. I got to know this short, likeable man who gave our radio a safe haven and whose weakness, according to Maria, was his love of girls. He strutted about like a peacock, head in the air, trying to present his best profile to the girls and to look taller. In later years, when I read about Mussolini, I would smile as I detected slight similarities between the vanity of the Duce and his underling in Athens. But unlike his superior in Rome, Colonel Cesarini was harmless and comical. When

I think of him now, Casanova, the dashing and egotistical Italian lover of the eighteenth century, comes to my mind, as if the Italians had run out of soldiers and so resurrected their legendary seducer of centuries past, hurriedly dressing him in uniform and sending him off to Athens to do his duty for his country. Or at least that may be how Cesarini saw himself.

When I was with Maria at the office one day she gave me some paper and colored pencils to keep me quietly occupied, and I set to work drawing. Combining my passion for aircraft with my patriotic fervor, I drew an aerial combat between English, German and Italian planes. My picture showed German and Italian planes crashing in flames while the British planes flew triumphantly above them. After a while I became aware of Colonel Cesarini standing behind me as I worked. Presently he called Maria over and muttered to her. She reddened as the Colonel prodded her to translate. "Mr Cesarini asked me," she said reluctantly, "to tell you that you have great talent but you're not fair. You should have some English planes shot down too, because that is how war is."

Cesarini smiled smugly, patted me on the shoulder and went about his business, evidently pleased at how adroitly he had handled things. My embarrassed sister warned me quietly to be more careful so as not to jeopardize her job.

When her job did end, and we lost the little financial support it had been bringing in, you wouldn't have thought it was a small loss if you'd judged by the numbers alone, for in the grotesquely devalued currency of the day Maria's tiny wages amounted to billions of drachmas. Anyone who had just about any money at all in Greece at that time was a billionaire.

• • •

Alexandra, the intellectual of our family, became engaged to be married. We'd wondered when this would happen. Many young men had tried to interest her but she was always too serious for romance and so aloof that we nicknamed her "The Countess". The man who finally won her heart was Nikos Symeonidis, who'd shared Dr Kapalas' basement air raid shelter on Mantzagriotaki and Lykourgou Streets while the bombs had fallen during the Italian attacks on Piraeus and other towns. Nikos lived around the corner from us on Lykourgou Street. He was at least ten years older than Alexandra, an educated businessman of superior intellect and, to my father's dismay, a communist. Their opposing political views inevitably led them into conflict. Our family wasn't alone in such dissension, for Greece, the crib of democracy, was by its deepest nature the home of vigorously opposed views representing every shade of the political and philosophical spectrum. The country's experiences in the twentieth century had created sharp divisions between people with increasingly polarized visions of the future. Nikos' entry into our lives thus reflected not only a stage in Alexandra's journey but a chapter in the chronicle of Greece. By the end of the war the differences between the country's various political groups were to explode in violence.

I was blissfully ignorant of these undercurrents of ideological tension between my elders. To me all that mattered about Nikos was his obvious love for my sister and the fact that he cared for me, too. He took me under his wing, reading me tales by Jack London, conversing with me and teaching me a good deal, including chess.

A newly somber note was creeping into Alexandra's life, though. We'd all grown weak from malnutrition but she looked the worst of us. She was very pale, coughed a lot and couldn't move easily. She withdrew into herself, sitting passively and managing at best to smile when others laughed. Nikos' friend Stamatiou, a doctor, examined her and grew grim. He, Nikos and my father conferred behind a closed door. After the doctor left my father told us Alexandra had tuberculosis, most likely in the most advanced stage. She urgently needed medication, better nourishment and clean air. There was nothing we could about the first two but with great effort my father and Nikos scraped together enough money to rent a small room in a place north of Athens called Agia Paraskevi. It was in open country with pine trees on the skirts of Mount Hymettus.

Our cousin Tota volunteered to accompany Alexandra. Tota had lost her engineer husband when his submarine, Triton, was sunk in 1942. She was an ideal companion, kind and helpful and funny. Even the loss of her husband hadn't suppressed her ability to come up endlessly with jokes. Once a week I went with Maria or Litsa to visit Alexandra, taking what food we could scrounge. Despite the relatively short distance it was an arduous trip. After taking the tram into Athens we boarded one of the city's few *gazozen*s, which chugged along at a snail's pace, and returned the same way. This went on for about six months when we ran out of money to pay Alexandra's rent and had to bring her home. I still wonder whether her stay there had any physiological advantage, since in those days there were hardly any cars around to pollute Kallithea's air. But sending Alexandra to the country made my family feel they were taking action, which was good for morale. As with the struggle in which Greece itself was enmeshed, it was vital to believe that victory was possible.

• • •

Greeks have always believed in the power of belief. Over thousands of years they've amassed a cornucopia of proverbs on this and every other subject, and one is: "Poverty needs a good time." This means poor people can and should enjoy their lives with whatever they have. In our case that meant that even in those desperate times we went to the movies once in a while.

The frequency of these treats varied throughout the war depended on our always slender means. In the early stages of hyperinflation the tickets were a few million drachmas, later rising to half a billion or more, but in terms of real buying power these amounts were tiny. Even so, our miserable budget didn't allow us to go very often. Yet everyone realized the importance of entertainment and distraction, so our family made every effort to retain our link with the make-believe of films.

Every Sunday Nikos took me by tram into Athens and we went to the Cineac theater, the only place then showing American movies. However, the Germans didn't allow live-action American movies; only black-and-white cartoons of Mickey Mouse, which for some reason the Germans considered acceptable. Walt Disney's creation became so familiar that Greeks came to refer to any movie cartoon as "Mickey Mouse".

Generally we could afford to send only two members of our family to see a movie, so to those lucky ones was entrusted the task of bringing the stories home to the rest of us. When they came home from the show the whole family gathered in our dining room and the two moviegoers related what they'd seen so everyone shared the entertainment. The story of the feature film was discussed with comments like "He shouldn't have done that" or "I would have followed my heart."

But children, though weaker than adults, have some resources that are unavailable to their elders, and while the rest of my family had to make do with the limitations on our movie attendance, I found another approach. When the open-air Palladion theater presented movies and live performers in summer I'd wait until it was dark, jump over the wall behind the screen and stealthily make my way among the seats until I found a vacant spot to claim. I engaged in this criminal behavior until 1944 and never got caught. If I had been, I doubt that any great penalty would have imposed on me, but the commando-like manner of my attendance gave my enjoyment of these shows an extra savor. Sneaking around somehow seemed fitting to wartime conditions.

• • •

Most of the live-action films we saw during the Occupation were German and Italian but we also had some French and Hungarian ones, as well as German propaganda such as the 1941 film *Kampfgeschwader Lützow* ("Battle Squadron Lützow"), which featured two heroic German bomber pilots, Eckhardt and Paulsen, in the Polish campaign and actions against the British Isles. Although these characters were our enemies I hoped they'd return home safely from their dangerous missions. But when we watched a film version of the Italian composer Puccini's opera *Tosca*, the audience applauded the escaped political prisoner Angelotti and booed his pursuer, the wicked police chief Scarpia, and in so doing we were really venting our feelings about the Occupation since we were rooting for freedom against uniformed wielders of power. But we were watching an officially permitted Italian film so there was nothing the Occupation censors could do about it.

I remember the Italian films as tending to be less about heroes and more about love. Many films left faces that still linger in my mind: the German actors Gustav Fröhlich, Theo Lingen and Marika Rökk; tenor Beniamino Gigli, singing the hit song Mamma, and his fellow Italians Alberto Rabagliati, the beautiful Alida Valli and a young, short and skinny Rossano Brazzi. Valli later made it into English-language films like *The Third Man* while Brazzi, still playing lovers even as he grew ever plumper, showed up after the war in Hollywood films like *Three Coins in the Fountain* and *South Pacific*.

• • •

The movies weren't only an escape for me but an education at a time when formal education had pretty much taken a back seat to survival and the functioning of schools had been disrupted by the war. Although I was already a lover of books, the films I saw stimulated my passion for reading even more, not only by making me interested to learn about the subjects of the films and by deepening my appreciation of story, but also by sharpening my reading skills. Since all the movies were foreign, they had subtitles. If you read too slowly, the caption changed before you read the whole thing. So if you wanted to keep abreast of the plot you had to read faster, and I did. Eventually I was able to absorb every caption in a flash before it changed. This movie-driven practice, together with my own extensive reading at home, was developing my verbal skills excellently. Nevertheless, our schoolteacher, Mrs Paleologou, decided to do something about what she regarded as the flagging education of her pupils. She couldn't give private lessons to my whole grade but she chose a few pupils whom she offered to teach if their parents could pay her a small fee. A few times a week in July of 1943 I went for lessons in her garden.

I think there were four other pupils: my friend Gianni, a boy called Sozon Antonatos, and two girls both called Nellie. I attended those classes with the same enjoyable sense of secrecy that I felt when I sneaked into the open-air movie theater, because Mrs Paleologou taught us with the standard reader for the third grade and I chose not to let her know that at home I'd already finished H. G. Wells' *The Invisible Man* and was now on Victor Hugo's *The Hunchback of Notre-Dame*.

I looked forward to those classes not for the reading but because they were an opportunity to socialize and, I now think, for the comfort of returning briefly to an environment that felt like school again. This was part of the benefit of going to the movies as well. People liked it not only because they could lose themselves in the lives of the characters on the screen but also because when they looked sideways they saw their friends and neighbors sitting around them, being entertained with them and sharing in a single experience that was peaceful and unthreatening, as things had been in the old days before the war. As if for a little while the world had gone back to normal.

• • •

One didn't see only friends and neighbors at the movies. The Germans came too. They attended only the open-air theaters that operated in summer, never the indoor cinemas. The idea of being cooped up in a dark hall surrounded by hostile Greeks must have made them nervous. They usually came in small groups and sat with their caps on their laps. There was an unspoken understanding between them and the rest of the audience. They ignored us and we ignored them. They were set apart from us not only by this avoidance of contact but by the spaces of empty seats that were always left around them. No matter where they sat there were always one or two empty seats between them and us. No Greeks wanted to sit next to them.

When the movies were German, the soldiers had an advantage over us because they laughed at the jokes or reacted to the turn in the drama before we had a chance to read the captions. But when the movies were Italian, French or Hungarian, we had the upper hand and they were the bewildered ones because these movies had no captions in German. To the rest of the audience there was always something satisfying in this.

However, such passive expressions of rebellion against the Occupation were increasingly giving way to more active opposition. People returning from the countryside told us how the Resistance organization ELAS was carrying out hit-and-run strikes against Germans and Italians, with their ranks swelling daily. More and more walls of houses were emblazoned with freedom slogans and the streets were littered with propaganda fliers. Only after the war would we learn that the printing press that produced many of these leaflets was hidden under the floorboards of a house just a few blocks from us. The desire to be free was asserting itself, as it has always done throughout history. Just as the images on our movie screens unfolded dramas and comedies in ways that the audience couldn't control, so the war was now on course to a resolution that wasn't of our invaders' choosing.

But the story would get rougher before it played out.

Italian troops advance on Albania.

Chapter 24 : Friends and enemies

One of my most haunting images of 1943 came neither from a movie nor from anything I saw but from an event which was described to my family by two of our neighbors who witnessed it.

The Germans needed to find new cannon fodder to fight the Russians on the Eastern Front after they suffered a devastating loss of men in their defeat by the Russians at Stalingrad, and word went about that they were poised to announce a conscription of Greeks. There had been a similar fear in late 1942 and Archbishop Damaskinos had sent a circular to be read in churches urging all Greeks to go on strike in protest. A mass strike followed: the entire male population stayed home, everything came to a standstill, and Kallithea became as quiet as a cemetery. The Germans must have been shaken by the solidarity and breadth of this expression of public antipathy because as far as I can recall the talk of conscription died away. But in 1943 a renewed wave of alarm about conscription arose in Kallithea, and once again my home and our street buzzed with public outrage.

The idea of families sending their menfolk into battle was awful enough on its own, but being compelled to do so on behalf of a hated invader was even worse. And a German draft would have been doubly catastrophic for households that had already lost fathers, husbands and sons in Albania. Men who feared German conscription had few choices, one of which was to leave their homes and join the swelling ranks of the Resistance in the mountains. This wouldn't enable them to elude the risk of death but at least it would be for their own people and not for a foreign power. They also had the option of fleeing to the British-controlled Middle East to attach themselves to some military or paramilitary unit there. Both routes were fraught with danger. Travel restrictions had been greatly tightened and the watchful eyes of the invaders and their spies made it increasingly difficult to reach the mountains, while traveling by boat anywhere in the greater Mediterranean region wasn't only hazardous but expensive as boat-owners wanted to be compensated handsomely for the peril to their craft and their lives. The hazards were very real and efforts to slip among the islands often ended in tragedy. My cousin from the island of Chios, Achileas Loizos, who'd fought in Albania, tried to escape in a dinghy to Turkey and was intercepted by a German patrol boat. We heard that his bullet-riddled body was found washed ashore on a Turkish beach.

When the reports of impending conscription surfaced afresh in 1943, thousands of Greeks flocked to the center of Athens where they held a mass demonstration aimed at showing the Germans just how massive the public reaction to this possibility was and would be.

I listened intently as our neighbors, Spyros Metaxas and Hippocrates Syrakos (one of our dining room generals) reported the demonstration to my father and the rest of us. Vivid in my mind to this day are their descriptions of the unarmed multitude facing German tanks. Most unforgettable of all was their account of how the forefront of the throng was made up of a large number of Greek amputees who'd been maimed in the war. These veterans had no wheelchairs but were borne on a variety of vegetable-vendors' carts. In the front ranks of the protest, more visible and thus more exposed to the German guns than any other demonstrators, they defiantly shouted anti-German slogans. As Spyro and Hippocrates recounted this dramatic day, tears rolled down my father's cheeks. Whether the Germans were also moved by the demonstration or whether they simply regarded the public outcry as once more too strong to make it worth their while to proceed with conscription, talk of this prospect again died away and we had no more of it.

• • •

On September 8, 1943, General Dwight D. Eisenhower, the Allies' Supreme Commander in the Mediterranean, announced that Italy had surrendered.

Marshal Pietro Badoglio was by then Italy's prime minister, Mussolini having been removed from power in July. The Allied invasion of mainland Italy was under way, plunging the country into confusion.

On September 12 German paratroopers rescued Mussolini from the mountain where his own people were holding him prisoner, and Hitler established him as head of a puppet government in northern Italy even as the Allied forces advanced from the south.

Alarmed at the prospect of Italian weapons and troops coming under Allied command, the Germans moved immediately to strip Italian soldiers of weapons, dealing savagely with any who resisted disarmament or showed signs of wanting to cross over to the Allied side. Italian blood flowed on Greek soil as a result: in several actions in late September the Germans massacred thousands of Italian soldiers of the Acqui Division occupying the Greek island of Cephalonia.

According to the London *Times*, when Allied forces occupied Italy's southern port of Reggio di Calabria it was practically deserted and they took it without having to fire a shot. *The Times* correspondent reported that the many captured Italian soldiers were "rejoicing and exuberantly trying to fraternize with their captors."

In Kallithea we heard later that many fully-armed Italian units in

Greece had joined our Resistance fighters in the mountains or cities to fight their former allies the Germans. Despite the war, there was no deep-seated enmity between Italians and Hellenes. Their histories and cultures had been intertwined for thousands of years, creating a framework of friendship that temporary phenomena like Mussolini and Hitler couldn't undermine. Some Italian soldiers sought refuge in the homes of forgiving Greeks who gave sanctuary to their defeated invaders and hid them from the Germans.

Years later I was to hear testimony about this time from my friend Marinos George. Earlier in 1943, before the German-Italian alliance was broken, he was working in the kitchen of a small taverna in the Greek town of Tripoli, still relying on the same skills he'd used as an army cook during the campaign against the Italians on Albania's snowbound mountains. The taverna was full of Greek customers and at one table four Italian soldiers sat eating quietly. They and the Greek customers ignored one another. Three German soldiers entered, boisterous because they'd been drinking. One of them, catching sight of the Italians, swaggered over to their table. Picking up one of their feathered hats, he used it to dust off his shoes.

Since these Italians whom the German had decided to humiliate were still at that time Germany's allies, the act of abasement was even more shocking than it might otherwise have been. The German roared with laughter and looked around at the Greek crowd to join him. After all, hadn't even Hitler praised the Greeks in their struggle against the Italians?

The taverna was silent. No one would join in this cruel humiliation of the Italians. All the Greeks sat staring at their plates, pretending not to see the boorish spectacle. After the Germans left, a Greek took a bottle of wine that had probably cost him a large portion of his wages and walked over to the Italians. Without a word, and not looking any of them in the eye, he set the bottle on their table and returned to his seat.

The story would be fine enough if it ended just there, but there's more to it that gives it even greater meaning. The Greek who presented the bottle of wine in consolation to the insulted Italians was called Panayotis, and my friend Marinos George knew him well. Panayotis, too, was a veteran of the campaign against the Italians in Albania. Marinos was aware that in a nightmarish charge up a hill, this man had suddenly found himself with a momentary power of life and death over two Italian soldiers. They knew as they looked into his eyes that in an instant he would decide whether or not to spare them. In their abject terror they cried out for mercy with terse words of supplication, *"Buono Greco! Buono Greco!"* ("O, kind Greek! O, kind Greek!") But the heat of desperate battle in defense of his country permitted Panayotis no time for compassion. When he stumbled away a moment later the blood of the two men was on his bayonet and on the snow.

Perhaps his gesture in that taverna in Tripoli in 1943, when without explanation he reached out his hand to restore the trampled dignity of those other soldiers of Italy, brought him peace. I hope so.

The Germans' orders to hunt down Italian soldiers in Greece brought to the fore not only the infinite potential of friendship and clemency but new possibilities of trade. For Italian fugitives who had no appetite to take up arms against their former allies but wanted simply to evade German wrath by disappearing into the Greek population, it was essential to have civilian clothes and, however little it was now worth, some money. In exchange they generally had something to offer, namely light weapons, ammunition and sundry small items of war materiel. Resistance groups in Kallithea and elsewhere conducted a lively business with the obliging Italians. It helped both sides:

survival for the Italians and more supplies for the Resistance fighters, who now redoubled their efforts to shake off the German yoke.

• • •

Our radio's reappearance on the small table in the dining room had not only brought us a resumption of our furtively accessed stream of news from the BBC; it also provided us with an early warning system for air raids. All radio stations in Greece went off the air the moment they were alerted of incoming aircraft, otherwise the pilots would be helped by being able to use the radio waves for guidance. So as soon as our *Er-Ce-Ah* fell silent we knew we had to take cover, even though The Chinaman hadn't yet begun to wail.

Our radio's homecoming also reinvigorated the dining room generals, who resumed their nightly strategic deliberations. The content of their discussions reflected the changing tide of the war. Their index fingers now traced imagined troop movements and strategic thrusts on those parts of the wall map that represented Italy and the Eastern Front. North Africa was no longer of interest because the Axis had been defeated there. This change in the Reich's fortunes, together with Italy's surrender and the disaster visited on the Germans at Stalingrad, also resulted in my overhearing remarks that were unaccustomedly optimistic.

"I think the war will be over by Christmas next year."

"I think it will be sooner. They cannot last that long."

It was Hippocrates, the group's political sage, who first introduced the bleak and paradoxical realization that good news for the Allied struggle against Germany wasn't entirely good news for Greece, at least not immediately.

"Now that the Allies are in Italy they will start bombing us," he observed. No one could disagree with his logic. It stood to reason that as long as Greece was under German control our roads and other infrastructure qualified as a target, since these amenities could be used by the Hitler to aid his war effort. Greece would thus very probably be bombed by those who were fighting to liberate Europe.

The dining room generals now scrutinized the map from this freshly dismaying perspective, speculating on likely targets and the range of Allied bombers based in Italy.

"I think their targets will be the port installations," someone ventured.

"Railroad depots are also strategically very important," remarked another.

So not only were our original invaders, the Italians, now fighting with the Greek Resistance and finding haven in Greek homes, but the dining room generals had shifted their focus from the threats to us posed by our German enemies to the coming destruction that we could expect to be rained upon us by our British and American friends. And strangely enough, although I recall many evenings in which they analyzed all the vulnerable parts of Greece that the Allies would damage – roads, bridges, ports, railroad deports and other installations – I don't remember them saying much about that which was most threatened of all. Perhaps they intentionally avoided mentioning it because the recognition of this point of vulnerability was so frightening.

It was us.

PART FIVE : DAYS OF FIRE

Chapter 25 : A BIG BALL OF FLAME

The era of bombing that now began was unlike the air raids we'd experienced earlier in the war, not only because of the psychological strangeness of being bombed by friends but also in the light of more practical differences both positive and negative. On the positive side there was a general feeling that the Allies wouldn't wish to inflict massive damage on Athens, a city containing so much of historical and cultural importance to the Western civilization that Britain and America were fighting to protect. On the negative side, there wasn't total certainty about this.

At an early stage in the war Greek authorities had declared Athens an open city, which meant it wouldn't be defended with military force. This was done to avoid exposing the city's historical and cultural treasures to damage. But with the Germans in charge of Athens, who could tell whether the previous open city declaration had any meaning for the advancing Allies? The Germans hadn't agreed that it was an open city and wouldn't do so until October 1944. Nobody in Greece was privy to Allied plans so there was no way of predicting whether the Allies would see some strategic advantage in knocking out some parts of Athens which they considered helpful to the Germans.

And even if central Athens were spared, the Allies might see the edges of the city's greater region differently. For example, the fact that Kallithea was a largely residential area hadn't spared us from needing air raid shelters earlier. And now we even had a German base in our midst; indeed, right across the road from our house. Who knew what this would mean for us? Finally, there was the critical fact that regardless of what happened or didn't happen to central

Athens, Kallithea was just a few miles from the port of Piraeus, which was most certainly a strategic target of considerable importance. Piraeus had been almost destroyed by the Germans in April of 1941, but by 1943, this time under German control, it was again among the prime targets. The US Army Corps of Engineers (which would help rebuild the damage after the war) would later sum it up thus: "Allied bombing raids destroyed miles of railroads and devastated the major port cities of Salonika, Volos, and Piraeus." To make matters even worse, when the Germans eventually pulled out they would first reduce to rubble key roads, bridges and parts of the Corinth Canal which linked Athens to the Adriatic Sea.

• • •

At first the air raids were sporadic. But they grew steadily more frequent, becoming an almost daily feature of our lives until the Germans left our mainland in October of 1944. Day and night the Americans and the British bombed us. The Chinaman, our siren on the roof of the Town Hall of Kallithea, howled incessantly. The BBC now warned the Greek population of Allied bombing, sometimes identifying specific targets around the Greater Athens area such as the airfields at Piraeus, Tatoi and Kalamaki and the naval installations at Skaramanga. Even when the targets weren't visible from Kallithea, like Skaramanga, we saw the flashes as the explosions lit up the sky.

Our reactions to all this varied over time. Initially we were unnerved. Then gradually the almost nightly repetition of these celestial displays numbed us so that it became routine. Yet even the protection of habit is limited and beneath the numbness there always lurked an awareness of the possibility of our own destruction. This was so for everyone, of every age, who had the mental ability to have some idea of what was happening. And we just had to live with these feelings.

But it's human nature to enjoy a show even when the audience is exposed to danger, and as with the bombings earlier in the war anxiety was always mitigated by fascination. The night raids were spectacular, eclipsing even the fireworks with which in happier times we'd celebrated the Resurrection of Christ at Easter. You'd think that with the possibility of being struck by a bomb or a burning piece of debris, everyone would take cover. But no, people were compelled to mill about in the streets and their gardens, utterly exposed as they gazed up in wonder at the entertaining performance and listening to the explosions.

• • •

The action would begin shortly after The Chinaman started his howling. The Germans turned on their searchlights and their piercing beams, I think about a dozen were visible from our house, moved to and fro scanning the sky for Allied planes like long probing fingers. When one of these shafts of light found a plane all the others quickly converged on it. The plane was then like a bird caught in a trap and the German anti-aircraft guns ("eighty-eights", for eighty-eight millimeters) started their fearsome pounding as they poured their firepower toward the illuminated target. Some of these guns must have been hidden in our vicinity because we had to cover our ears.

From what I was told, it was the Royal Air Force's De Havilland Mosquitos, the "spotters", that came first in these raids, pinpointing the target with magnesium flares that briefly turned night into day. The flares were attached to parachutes measuring about a foot across; these descended slowly while the flare burned, dispelling the blackout with a widespread glow that was so bright we could see each the details of each others' upturned faces in sharp relief. There was only a small interval of darkness between the flares because they were dropped in rapid succession. The Mosquito pathfinders were followed by the heavy bombers, the Lancasters, which did the destructive work.

My grandmother, who'd by then rejoined the family from Leonidion, was the only person I can recall who had the sense to hide from this pandemonium, going behind a big armoire to pray for divine protection. It occurred to me in later years that perhaps she wasn't really so sensible, though, because the armoire had heavy glass doors and I wonder whether she ever considered what might happen to her if a blast shattered them.

• • •

The anti-aircraft artillery used tracer ammunition that left incandescent trails of red, green and yellow in the air and these appeared to us to climb slowly toward the plane and simply disappear when they reached their target. It was a very different experience for the airmen on the receiving end when the shells burst, scattering shrapnel of every size. I witnessed only one such strike. There was a big ball of flame in the sky, then darkness.

"They got him," someone said.

"Just imagine his poor mother," said another.

I realized in later years that planes of the kind making those bombing raids would have had crews of several men, and I wonder today whether all of them died in the ball of fire I saw. Perhaps survivors, or at least even just one survivor, parachuted safely to the ground, went into hiding and eventually made it back home. I like to think so.

• • •

Apart from the columns of smoke that the dawn revealed after a raid, there were other grim reminders of the night's havoc. After a raids I'd go out hunting for the little flare parachutes and I found quite a few. I tied rocks on them and threw them from our terrace to re-enact their original descent in my macabre imagination. There were also other trophies. Occasionally during a raid we heard a bit of an aircraft thud into the ground and every morning I scoured the area for these fragments. By the end of the war I had box of them, of all shapes and sizes, all razor-sharp with jagged edges.

Our storytelling neighbor Mr Hadjimihalis, whose relatives had thought Halley's Comet meant doomsday, told us of a girl who was watching the air raids when a piece of metal fell from the sky and cut off one of her fingers. During the next air raid she was again outside to take in the panorama, this time with a bandage on her hand. I don't know whether this really happened or whether it was a cautionary fable intended to instill some wisdom into us. Either way it had not the slightest educational effect. We all laughed and the next night we were out in the middle of the street again to admire the lethal lights in the sky, ignoring the peril to our lives.

My father, with his real military experience, taught me how to calculate the distance of an explosion. "The minute you see the flash, you start counting the seconds until you hear the sound. Then you then count how many seconds." But that's all I ever absorbed. I was apparently like the rest of the human race, enthralled by war as well as afraid of it, but reluctant to learn from it.

• • •

I gathered from listening to my elders that for some reason the British tended to conduct the night raids while the Americans ran things during the day. Without the pitch-black sky as a backdrop, the daytime visits were much less breathtaking. They were also much deadlier. One of our dining room generals commented: "They have too many bombs and don't know what to do with them, so they drop them on us." But perhaps it was just easier to see the targets by day. It was certainly easy for me to see the planes in the clear, cloudless skies. As I recall, American planes that flew missions over our region weren't painted. They were gleaming silver specks that left white vapor trailing behind them. When the German guns hammered away at them we couldn't see the tracers in the daylight but a lot of little black smoke puffs appeared around the planes and in front of them as the shells exploded. Still, the planes kept going until they dropped their bombs on targets like Piraeus, then they headed seaward and disappeared.

Our neighbor Mr Malatestas, of the dining room generals, had a two-story house and from his terrace my father's binoculars enabled me to see across the Plain of Attica as far as the airfields at Tatoi and Kalamaki. I watched big geysers of dirt erupt in the air and the smoke unfurl from the explosions. I didn't conduct this surveillance alone. Three houses from us, on another terrace, German officers were doing the same thing. A couple of times they trained their binoculars on me and I suppose they saw that I was a child, for nothing was done about my watching. Maybe one or two of them even recognized me as that annoying Greek boy who was always around their camp or even inside their barbed-wire perimeter.

• • •

In October of 1943 our nightly BBC access came under threat yet again. The Germans turned their attention afresh to the existence of "rogue" radio users listening to banned broadcasts. This renewed German concern may have been fueled by the fact that BBC broadcasts now included cryptic sentences like "the moon is blue" or "the dog has three legs", whose apparently meaningless phrases were believed to mask messages to the Greek Resistance. There were also messages that seemed to be from Greek men based with Allied fighting units in Egypt: "Giannis sends his love to Grigori and Maria", "Tell Eleni that Kostas is well and sends his love", and so on. Perhaps the Germans objected to the morale-lifting effects such messages might have, or perhaps they suspected that these, too, were coded communications to the Resistance.

In any event the newspapers published a dire final warning that anyone possessing an unsealed radio, capable of receiving transmissions from any broadcaster other than the German-controlled radio station in Athens, had one last chance to surrender it for sealing. The penalty for failing to do so was a free train ride to a concentration camp in Germany, or worse. The Germans later announced that some forty-three thousand people had complied, although it's hard to know what to make of this claim because there was no reason to believe any of their propaganda. But whether forty-three thousand complied or forty-three, my father wasn't among them. He stood his ground and we continued to live precariously as outlaws of the airwaves, with our *Er-Ce-Ah*'s integrity preserved.

The intimidating tone of the Germans' final warning wasn't without its effect in our house, however. This time the decision of the dining room War Council to continue defying the Germans was not unanimous, as it had been in the past. Half the generals voted to ignore the radio ultimatum. The other half voted to comply. Since it was my father's radio and his house, he had the deciding vote and so prevailed. But the reservations that had divided the generals over this issue couldn't be overlooked and a mood of heightened strain now settled on the group. Although the discussions of the nightly news persisted it was with a more guarded enthusiasm and in more subdued voices

{ 231 }

which, when they fell almost to whispers, reflected not only the need for security but also the fact that the latest German ultimatum had taken its toll. The atmosphere was no longer the same.

• • •

These questions of life and death continued to mingle in our minds with the practical problems of daily existence as winter approached. For example, my lack of shoes. School was about to reopen but my sandals with the twisted rope soles were unsuitable for the cold and the mud puddles. A solution was found, but it didn't delight me. Back in 1939 my mother had bought me a pair of galoshes, rubber rain boots designed to be worn over one's shoes and not in place of them, which is precisely how I now had to wear them. They were too big so we stuffed them with newspaper. My feet didn't like this. Every evening my sisters had to massage them because, for reasons we couldn't understand, being enclosed in boots stuffed with newspaper made them swell. Nevertheless I went to school like this until 1945. When my feet grew sufficiently to fit into the galoshes without padding I just removed the newspaper.

Shoes were by no means all that we lacked. Over the three years or so of war we'd been unable to replace any cups, glasses, plates and dishes that had been broken, cracked or chipped in the normal wear and tear of use, so where necessary we used Red Cross sardine cans as food containers. They came in two shapes: flat oval ones which we used as plates and cylindrical ones that served as makeshift cups. Unfortunately no amount of washing could do away with their smell of fish, which infused everything we ate out of them for the first week or two of use in their new capacities. We shrugged and got used to it.

The only large plate we had by then was a British army-issue aluminum plate that we used as our general serving dish. It had been given to my father by a departing British liaison officer at The Barracks shortly before the Germans entered Athens. I think it was part of a mess kit. My father would continue to use it as his personal plate for the rest of his life, giving it pride of place over the fancy china that was to come back into our home. A few years before this book was produced, one of my sisters found this battered old plate in a cupboard and gave it to me. It is pitted by time and when I look at it I wonder what British soldier used it, and what he ate from it as he thought of home and of whether he'd ever see his loved ones again. I wonder through what battles this plate passed and whether it had only one user until it came into my father's hands or whether it passed from soldier to soldier as its owners fell to the bullets and shells of the Third Reich. Most of all, I wonder what inexpressible private feelings tugged at my father's breast as he ate his meals in those years after the war, when, each time he scraped away his last morsel, he looked down at the worn surface that quietly reflected back at him more memories than the pen can tell.

German paratroops of 5 Gebirgs-Division boarding a Junkers 52 at a Greek airfield, before flying to Crete, 20 May 1941. On that morning 3000 German paratroops landed at Maleme, Rethymno, Chania and Heraklion.

Bundesarchiv: Bild 146-1980-090-34 / photographer unknown

CHAPTER 26 : *AN ENEMY OF MY OWN*

Despite the air raids and the uncertainty as to what the Germans would do next in response to the Allied campaign, we entered 1944 on a note of hope. Although the war was far from over, Hitler was suffering vast reverses. Our *Er-Ce-Ah* informed us nightly that the Russians were relentlessly chasing the Germans across the steppe while the Anglo-American alliance advanced more slowly but nonetheless steadily into Italy. And our Red Cross rations, while scanty, were at least coming in regularly. In addition, January 1944 was unusually mild and the sun was balm to our undernourished bodies and battered spirits. All we had to do, it appeared, was hang on a little longer. Spring was around the corner and freedom only a little farther down the road.

However, 1944 turned out to be one of the bloodiest of the Occupation. It was a time of horror, mass executions and the burning of entire communities and towns, and the twists and turns of history were taking it toward a new kind of chaos in which Greek would eventually turn on Greek. I not only witnessed some of this bedlam but escaped with my life only by slipping through the narrowest cracks of chance and circumstance.

Much of 1944 is a blur of impressions in my memory now but if I were pressed to choose a point at which that deceptively hopeful season flared into a freshly kindled bonfire of catastrophe, it would have to be January 11, a warm, sunny Tuesday. On that day the port of Piraeus, which had already been hit hard in previous raids, was subjected to a tremendous new air assault, this time by American bombers. When The Chinaman started wailing I grabbed my father's binoculars and headed to Mr Malatestas' terrace. I knew it was the Americans because the British came only at night. Sure enough, the gleaming silver B17 Flying Fortresses were all over the sky, their fluffy cotton-like contrails hanging in the blue behind them. They flew over Piraeus and dumped everything they had on the port. They kept coming in waves for, I think, some three hours.

While we saw the planes and heard the explosions, we in Kallithea had no way of knowing the details of what was happening in Piraeus. We were able to put together a picture of events only later when we listened to radio reports and first-person accounts given to us in shaking voices by the streams of shocked people from Piraeus who poured into Kallithea seeking help and refuge. We gathered from the stories of these broken people that for some extraordinary reason the Americans had left the German-held naval station and shipyards untouched: their bombs had fallen on the working-class districts of Drapetsona, Kaminia and Tabouria, which had been populated in the twenties by thousands of refugees from the Greco-Turkish War.

Flames had consumed the residents' homes, schools and small businesses. It was reported that hundreds of Greeks had died, over a thousand injured, thousands left homeless.

The Germans claimed they'd lost eight soldiers.

• • •

Many Kallitheans were commuters who worked in Piraeus, so large crowds gathered anxiously at the Kallithea tram station to look for their loved ones in anxious hope that they would return safely. Their distress was amplified by the alarming condition of the multitude of survivors brought in by every vehicle from Piraeus. We were told they were thronging from the station in hundreds, their clothing tattered and some with burns and other injuries. Mingling with the returning Kallitheans, who were greeted with tears of relief by their families, were newly uprooted residents of Piraeus, for whom history was cruelly repeating itself by once more reducing them to refugees as their families and communities had been in the nineteen-twenties after the war in Asia Minor. Again they were seeking shelter with some relative or charitable stranger.

These people came with little or nothing more than what they wore, for the air raid had allowed them no time to retrieve their possessions if they wished to get out with their lives. Most brought with them not even the precious ration coupons that would secure them some Red Cross food. Kallitheans had to share with this displaced population what little food we had. For me, though, this influx of newcomers also meant that I acquired another half a dozen or so playmates in the neighborhood: the children of destitute evacuees. It was thus to a somewhat different Kallithea that spring and summer came in 1944. Whereas starvation had previously thinned our community, there were now new faces on which was written the heartbreak of a smoldering Piraeus.

With friends new and old I went as before into the fields to harvest the nettles which, together with the Red Cross food served at school, provided enough sustenance, more or less, to enable me to maintain my attention in the classroom, be introduced to the world of fractions and decimal values, and learn more patriotic songs. I even had energy left for street games. But while school, the improved weather and the excitement of new friends and neighbors gave me welcome distractions from the tensions of our lives, it was impossible not to be aware of the added strain in my elders' eyes and in the conversations that I overheard. The Piraeus calamity appallingly confirmed that the turning of the tide of war against Germany didn't necessarily mean the waning of our problems, but could, in at least the immediate term, bring us even worse ones.

And this is indeed how it turned out.

• • •

The scents and brilliant colors of spring and summer blossoms now engulfed our neighborhood but even this profusion of tenderness and beauty couldn't mask the smell of blood that the Piraeus fugitives had infused into the households of Kallithea. Although death had called on our area before, it had done so quietly and not through mass destruction, which Kallithea had been spared despite the frightening air raids we'd experienced earlier in the war. But the prospect of losing home and personal belongings and the fragile forms of security to which my elders clung to make their lives bearable, and possibly of being killed, was now closer and more real than ever before. And just as the bombing of Piraeus was made more horrific and perplexing by the fact that it had been perpetrated not by the Germans but by the Americans who were fighting Hitler, so now a new moral and psychological weight descended on the shoulders of my elders regarding the role of the Greek Resistance. This role was essential to the Greek spirit and supportive of the Allied struggle to end the Third Reich, and it was also unstoppable. But it was also a source of increasing fury among the Germans.

Resistance actions were expanding daily. Although my family and I and our neighbors didn't know the identities of those members of our community who were actively working for the Resistance, since this information came out only after the war, there was a general awareness that Resistance workers lived among us. Anybody, even the seemingly least heroic person, could be a Resistance fighter. After the war we learned that people we would never have thought capable of such risk-taking were among the heroes of the Resistance.

• • •

The Germans responded with bestial ferocity to the increased Resistance actions. This added a new level of suspenseful worry to everyday life in our community. It was impossible to predict either Resistance actions or what the Germans would do to retaliate, especially since the elusiveness of the Resistance meant the Germans tended to take their rage and frustration out on the general population. They were becoming more and more unstable and unpredictable, like a cornered wild animal. They were, in fact, now being cornered at last by the successes, combined might and determination of their foes. The German mailed fist consequently came down viciously on Greece's civilians. Arrests, raids, executions, the torture of interrogated prisoners and the sudden disappearance of friends and neighbors became common in the atmosphere of intimidation that now prevailed.

The latest German reprisals, or the ones that it was feared they would soon carry out, become a main topic of conversation in our neighborhood. Whenever people met, the conventional greetings would quickly and inevitably give way to talk about some new German atrocity, verified or rumored. Where the details were unclear this often made it worse. People known and unknown to us just disappeared. One shuddered when imagining what had been done to the vanished ones by the Gestapo or the Schutzstaffel, the Nazi organization known by its twin lightning-bolt SS insignia.

One of the most chilling things to hear about anyone was that he or she had been taken to Haidari, a prison on the slopes of Mount Aigaleo run by the SS as a transfer center from which detainees were shipped to the death camp Auschwitz, in an area of Poland which Germany had annexed, or to slave labor camps in Germany. Executions and torture took place at Haidari and its name was spoken in undertones, as were the phrase "Number Six" and the word Kessariani. Number Six Merlin Street in central Athens, known just by its number, was the headquarters of the Gestapo. This mansion in the exclusive Athens suburb of Kolonaki was a symbol of menace and foreboding; one of the most hopeless things that could be said of any Greek was that he or she was at Merlin Street. Unspeakable things happened behind those doors and few prisoners came out in one piece.

Kessariani was an area north of Athens which, like Drapetsona, Kaminia and Tabouria, had grown out of a refugee camp for war exiles from Asia Minor in the twenties. The Germans saw it as a Resistance enclave and made it their business to spread terror among the residents. On May 1, at a rifle range there, the Germans massacred some two hundred Greeks. The name Kessariani thereafter struck fear into everyone and fanned rumors and speculations as to what similar slaughter the Reich was poised to inflict.

"Did you hear what happened in Kokkinia?" one neighbor would somberly ask another. "The Germans burned half the houses and executed seven hundred men and women of the Resistance. The blood was flowing on the streets."

"Have you heard? They burned the houses at Sfageia and shot a lot of people."

And so on and so on, including the names of missing people and endless invocations of the dread names of Merlin Street and Haidari, interspersed with deep sighs and weeping.

• • •

In late July of 1944 the German crackdown made itself felt in our own neighborhood when violence erupted on Bizaniou Street, some five blocks from us. The rattle of machine gun burst across the neighborhood and mortar shells exploded, and word later went around that ten Resistance fighters had lost their lives. I had some connection with this drama in that it took place on the premises of my school and the house where these young lives had ended was that of one of my teachers. We learned that the young men had been caught sleeping in the school. The tragedy of their deaths was deepened by the fact that their attackers included men of their own country who had given themselves over to the service of the Germans. These were a unit of the so-called Security Battalions, a military force made up of Greeks who collaborated with the Nazi Occupation, and members of the German-controlled Gendarmerie. We were told that when the youths of the Resistance were trapped they sought refuge with Mrs Megas, a widow who lived on Bizaniou Street just around the corner from the school. She was in the house with another lady and two children. The place was surrounded by German army units, the Security Battalions and the Gendarmerie. The boys fought, it was said, for five hours, repulsing the Germans and their collaborators, many of whom were killed or wounded. They besieged group then raised a flag of truce and asked for safe passage for the women and children. The Germans agreed on condition that one of the Resistance fighters surrendered. One did, and they shot him on the spot. The rest continued the battle until around noon, when, with only one bullet left to each, they committed suicide rather than fall into the hands of the enemy.

When I heard the name of the leader of this Resistance group I realized I knew him by sight. He lived in the slums of the Harokopou area. He was nineteen years old. The eldest of his group was twenty.

• • •

As we moved further into 1944 we again started running out of food. The distribution of Red Cross rations became irregular, then stopped, presumably because the shifting pattern of combat between the Allies and the Germans hindered Red Cross delivery. It was still possible to find food on the black market but only with British gold sovereigns, jewelry or bartering, all of which were beyond our means.

My grandmother, our Yaya, strengthened our survival efforts with her genius for culinary improvisation. She could combine the doubtful with the impossible and manage to come up with the edible. One day my father brought home from his foraging a single potato. I don't remember where he found it or even whether I was told its origin. Perhaps he'd pilfered it from a German truck. All I know is that the sight of this one potato was a marvel to me as by then I hadn't seen a potato for a couple of years or so. Yaya found a few drops of oil, which may have come from our Singer sewing machine, and fried the potato, half for my tubercular sister Alexandra and half for me. My taste buds remembered the luxury of fried potatoes instantly.

Despite all our hardships we clung to what we could of our summer routine of old, with all the neighborhood conspiring in a kind of collective pretense that things weren't that bad. As in summers past I played around barefoot all day, the chairs came out on the sidewalk in the afternoon, neighbors strolled along the street greeting each and stopping to pass the time of day. Eleni the piano teacher in the house of widows played her seasonal repertoire of classical music while the rest of us, even the Germans, listened mesmerized as before. In the evening, the young boys serenaded the girls with guitars and love songs as they had in summers past, slipping in a patriotic song here and there to defy the Germans. And I, sitting on the steps, listened to the adults discussing the never-ending ordeal. For distraction I turned my thoughts elsewhere, looking at the bright stars in the summer sky, imagining things I no longer remember.

• • •

The adherence to routine as a way of bolstering morale wasn't peculiar to us. The Germans did it too. Any time they had a major setback in the war, especially on the Eastern Front, they held a parade. They started from the Sivitanidios technical school and goose-stepped through our neighborhood singing martial songs. It was a great show of bravado but they didn't fool us. We now all knew that the days of overlordship left to them were short, even though we didn't know the precise number. The BBC was telling us of the Allies' push into France and how the Russians were closing in on Germany from the east. The generals in our dining room studied the map on the wall, drew conclusions, slapped one another on the back and spread the news in the neighborhood that we could justifiably hope for an end to the war in the not too distant future.

I now seldom saw my German "friends", Arthur and Alfred, and waited in vain for them to come out and play football with me. Instead, I acquired a German enemy of my own. His name was Willy.

He was short and swarthy with dark hair combed back and plastered on his scalp. I didn't like him. Once he killed a cat, skinned it, cut off its tail and head and tried to sell it as rabbit meat. Unlike Arthur and Alfred he always scooted me away from their camp. I was afraid of him and gave him a wide berth. But one boy in our neighborhood, a little older than I, confronted Willy without fear. A refugee from Stalin's Russia, he polished shoes for whatever he could get. In his entrepreneurial zeal he tried to drum up business with the Germans. One day Willy told him to move on. After retreating to a safe distance he showed his opinion of Willy by boldly throwing rocks at him, to my great if apprehensive admiration. Willy reciprocated in kind with more accuracy. Wisely, the urchin moved out of range and from this new point of attack he launched a tirade of verbal abuse not merely at Willy but against Hitler himself. His flood of invective included every obscene word in his vocabulary, which was impressively large. It was clear from Willy's expressions and body language that although he understood little or no Greek he recognized the name of his Führer and got the drift. So you could say the skirmish ended in a draw. Willy wasn't injured but it certainly seemed to me that he'd gained nothing in dignity from the exchange. It was, in its way, not a bad summing-up of the antagonism between Russia and Germany. At the time, of course, it was just another street incident to me.

Yet even children have thoughts about life and its larger currents, and when I lay in bed on those summer nights of 1944, the sounds and sights and feelings of the war whirled in every corner of my mind, and among them, as I drifted off to sleep, were always questions. I had questions about all the great forces which, according to my elders, controlled our destiny. I had questions about the mythical Olympian gods whose stories Alexandra so lovingly told me. I had questions about the God whom our priests praised in our Church, telling us that we were His children and that He loved us. I had questions about why it seemed that all these awesome and majestic shapers of our fate had reached a secret covenant to exterminate us.

CHAPTER 27 : *A GUN TO MY HEAD*

As our lack of food grew critical, my father appealed for help to Mr Konstantinidis, a banker whose wife had been my mother's best friend and whose children were my sisters' friends. It was agreed that I'd join Mr Konstantinidis' family for a month at their summer home at Alimos, an undeveloped seaside area beside the airfield at Kalamaki. Their villa was less than half a mile from the sea. Every day we walked down a dusty unpaved road to spend most of the morning on the beach, and some evenings too, although in late afternoon we returned to the villa for a siesta. I couldn't yet swim but I enjoyed splashing around in the sun and soon tanned to a dark brown. Lambis, the family's son of twenty or so, was always with me. He was a fine swimmer and took me into deep water on his shoulders so I could join him and his friends in games.

It was a sign of the tempo of the war that although the Luftwaffe still used the Kalamaki airfield I saw only one or two planes, dark Messerschmitt 109 fighters, land there during my month at the villa. I loved planes, regardless of whose they were, and never tired of asking questions about them. I was told the airfield was so desolate because the Reich had recalled most of its planes to defend Germany. I was greatly excited whenever I saw a lone Messerschmitt near the fenced perimeter of the airfield, revving its engine for take-off. I waved to the pilot and he lifted his gloved hand in greeting; for an instant we were like old friends in the brotherhood of the air.

One day, however, our proximity to the airfield, from which I drew so much pleasure, gave rise to one of the most frightening moments I'd ever know.

• • •

Guests were staying with us that week: a Mrs Kasidoris and her daughter Voula, about Lambis' age. It was a very hot July night and Lambis had left a couple of days before to help his father in Athens, a fortuitous coincidence that, as it turned out, may have saved his life. Having eaten our Red Cross meal, we got ready for bed. Most of us had mattresses on the floor. The bedtime routine was governed by the especially strict blackout enforcement in Alimos, where only the narrow, dusty road to the beach separated the villa from the airfield. There was an iron rule: only when all the lights were out was it permissible to open the blackout shutters and let the sea breeze in before getting into bed.

I went through this ritual before lying down on my mattress, but after a few minutes I remembered something, I can't now recall what, that I'd meant to find before going to sleep. I got up and groped around for it in the dark and when I couldn't lay hands on it I instinctively turned on the light. It took me just seconds to find whatever I was looking for and I switched the light off again immediately and returned to bed. But a few minutes later another overlooked chore occurred to me, so I repeated the procedure: light on, poking around the room for a few seconds, then light off again. I did all this without thinking to close the blackout shutters, as once more I did what I wanted to do in seconds. It didn't dawn on me that having the lights on for this tiny amount of time would bother anyone.

I was horribly wrong.

I was just nestling down into the first layer of sleep, in the twilight between consciousness and dreams, when suddenly a terrific eruption shook the villa from roof to floor. A thunder of running feet burst on my ears. The violent thumping of hobnailed boots reverberated through the house, climbing the marble staircase, clattering on the tiled floors everywhere. A cacophony of German voices at top volume, made all the more terrifying because they were mad with rage, barked orders amid female screams. It all happened so fast that the commotion penetrated into me and bore me along with it like a flood even before I had time to wake up properly.

Somebody rushed into my dark bedroom. It was Voula Kasidoris. She lifted my cover, crawled in and pulled the sheet over our heads to snuggle against me, convulsed with panic. I had no idea what was happening and had scarcely any time to wonder. Boots crashed into the room and a blaze of light blinded me even though my eyes were closed and under a bedsheet. My heart wanted to jump out of me. Wary but heavy, decisive steps approached. Voula quaked uncontrollably beside me. The sheet was ripped away and I squinted into the enormous barrel of a black gun. In a flash I saw it was the same kind my father had brought home and allowed me to hold briefly before locking it away: a Luger Parabellum. It was six inches or so from my forehead. There was a smell of oil, reminiscent of our Singer sewing machine at home.

Behind the Luger the glittering eyes of a German officer glared balefully down at me as he knelt on the parquet floor, his left hand poised in the air above me holding the end of the sheet. I pressed my eyes shut tight and held my breath, the way I always did before a firecracker went off.

An eternity of heart-pounding seconds passed. I opened my eyes. The officer was still inspecting Voula and me but with a different look. Perhaps, it occurred to me later, he was relieved not to be confronting an armed Resistance fighter. Some of the tautness left his glowering face as he returned his pistol to its leather holster and stood up. From my supine position he rose to tower over us like a monstrous giant of fable in his glistening boots, green-gray uniform and high peaked cap. He then did something that would have startled me afresh had I not been already struck numb. He bent over us, his great face descending from the lofty height to which it had receded, and he drew the sheet back over us to cover as completely as we had been before. I lay motionless, Voula trembling beside me, as the sound of his boots withdrew across the room, pausing only as he turned the light off on his way out.

We remained precisely as we were for some time until the house became quiet. Then, with the shutters securely closed and the lights on again, everyone, family and guests alike, gathered in the kitchen where a new ordeal awaited me. Mrs Konstantinidis didn't have a Luger to brandish at me but the barrage of wrath with which she bombarded me was ample and could hardly have been less frenzied than the passion with which the Germans had stormed the house. Her ire poured upon me with blistering hysteria. She accused me of almost having her son killed by the stupidity of my blackout violation.

It appeared that the on-off-on-off lights in my room, with the shutters open, had been seen at the airfield as a signal to Allied spotter planes to help target their bombs. The Germans had instantly dispatched a unit of armed soldiers who broke the villa's door down and searched the house to find the Resistance member sending the signals. Had they come across any adult male, especially Lambis, who was the right age for active Resistance participation, he would almost certainly have been arrested and perhaps never seen again. Fortunately the Germans believed Mrs Konstantinidis' explanation and left with a warning of serious repercussions if we broke the blackout rules again.

Of course it wasn't lost on me that in addition to putting Lambis at risk of imprisonment, torture and death, I myself could easily have been shot, and Voula too, if only by accident on the part of the nervous soldiers.

To compound my shame, the villa now had a hole where the front door had been, for the door had been battered loose from its hinges. It was heavy and everyone had to pitch in to lift it and rest it against the jamb until someone could be found to fix in the next few days. And while the door was being put into place, and even after that until I went to bed, I had to listen to Mrs Konstantinidis' reproaching me on and on for what I had almost done to her only son. I said nothing.

And I suddenly had this in common with so many other Greeks of those years, of all ages: I now knew what it meant to have a gun held to my head.

That night was also the beginning of a new dimension in my developing comprehension of my father. It would be years before I understood him fully, but dimly, slowly, clumsily, I was beginning to fathom why in his passion and urgency and desperation he had felt that if he could lock away even just a single Luger, so that it could not be pointed at any man, or at any woman like my mother, or at any girl like my sisters, or at any boy like me, that was something.

It was one less Luger in the world.

• • •

It must have been the beginning of August 1944 when I left the summer villa to return to Kallithea and my family. The nearest tram station was at Paleon Phaliron, two and a half to three miles from Alimos. Since no buses were running, Lambis walked me there along the coastal road. This was risky for him: by then people of his age were trying to keep out of sight as much as possible, for the Germans were randomly taking hostages to be shot in reprisal whenever one of their own was killed.

It was a very hot day. All along the road German trucks and many captured English Bedford trucks were parked behind barbed wire strung with tin cans containing pebbles. These served as a makeshift warning system since any intruder disturbing the fence would send a tremor rippling down the wire fence, rattling the pebbles in the cans to alert the guards. We walked past a group of soldiers firing live cannon shells continuously at a big balloon towed by a boat out at sea. They were practicing for an expected invasion of Greece by the Allies. After making sure I had the few million drachmas for the fare home Lambis began his walk back to the villa, leaving me to await the tram to Kallithea.

I returned home to find that the food crisis persisted. But home is home and it was good to be back. Although I was acutely aware that many threats were weighing heavily on my elders, from a child's point of view much in my life remained carefree. I roamed the streets all day, barefoot and bare-chested, playing with friends or getting into mischief. I left no street unexplored, no tree unclimbed, no wall unscaled, no neighbor's feathers unruffled.

As we huddled around our *Er-Ce-Ah* in the evenings we learned more of the Allies' advance into France as well as news of a failed attempt to kill Hitler. But whereas the Führer's days hadn't yet ended, our clandestine evenings with the BBC finally had. The bulletin about the unsuccessful assassination bid was the final broadcast that our beloved old radio brought us. Our *Er-Ce-Ah* was our last remaining possession of any value that could be used for barter. A man came to our house, talked with my father, wrapped the radio in a cloth, put it in a bag, and left. As payment he gave us half a bag of flour and a couple of pints or so of adulterated olive oil. Used sparingly, these items could keep us going for several weeks.

We never saw our *Er-Ce-Ah* again. An era in the life of our family was over.

• • •

Despite the now irrevocable loss of our radio, the dining room generals went on with their nightly meetings at our house. Although their information came only from rumor now, they maintained an abiding faith in their ability to comprehend the progress of the war. They persevered with their speculative discussions, analyses and conjectures as to the belligerents' likely battle strategies, studying the wall map together as intensely as ever, even though the movements of troops and aircraft that their fingers now traced upon it were derived wholly from their imaginations. Perhaps now more than ever, with the precious BBC connection lost, their morale crucially depended on their belief that they could deduce, by sheer logic alone, what was going on in the combat theaters of Europe.

"All we have to do now is stick it out. We'll celebrate victory with the English soon," one of them remarked. To which Hippocrates Syrakos snorted cynically and asked: "Why do you think they call it Perfidious Albion?"

I would one day learn that "Perfidious Albion", a phrase used in European literature, meant "treacherous Britain", in reference to various episodes in history when Britain was deemed to have been deceitful in its dealings with other nations. ("Albion" is an ancient name for Britain.) But although I wasn't familiar with the details of Hippocrates' intellectual reading at the time, I understood enough from his many past comments at our dining room table to know that he was very skeptical about the trustworthiness of the Allies, especially Britain. For example, he'd previously voiced suspicion of the motives and honesty of Britain's Prime Minister, Winston Churchill.

My father was more optimistic and didn't like these periodic expressions of negativity about "our Allies", so he gave Hippocrates a dirty look when he made his "Perfidious Albion" crack.

But events would show that Hippocrates had reason to raise the questions that he did.

• • •

The Allies kept up their air raids day and night. One night we were all in the street under the latest bright shower of magnesium flares descending slowly from the sky, creating an eerie glow of nocturnal daylight. The target was yet again the Skaramanga naval installations and everyone cheered with every flash and explosion as if we were at a fireworks display. The only person who hadn't come out into the street was my arthritic grandmother, who sat on our front steps to watch the performance in the sky. Suddenly, perhaps in a lull between blasts, there was a shout around the corner, followed by a torrent of German cries and two gunshots. We scattered. Doors slammed, leaving an emptied street. We didn't leave our house again that night. Later we gathered that the shooting had been intended to drive us indoors: our German neighbors had simply had enough of listening to us cheer for the Allies.

The next morning I discovered that one of the shots the Germans had fired to scare us into silence had chipped off a large chunk of the steps of Mrs Metaxas' house next door to us. This meant the bullet must have passed our front steps where Yaya had sat. When we discussed this it came out that my grandmother had gone inside for a glass of water only moments before the shooting began.

• • •

Alexandra, now weak and with her lungs half destroyed, was struck with tubercular peritonitis and writhed in pain, silently suffering day and night without complaining because she didn't want to upset us. No medicines were available. All we could do was put hot compresses with alcohol on her stomach, which we had to stop doing when her skin started peeling. Then the pharmacy ran out of alcohol and all we could give Alexandra was the comfort of our love. Out of her sight we wept.

In August Maria, too, fell ill. The doctor diagnosed typhus and my father and Litsa took her to the municipal hospital in central Athens. She could walk only with the two of them supporting her. The hospital doctors admitted that while they'd do their best they couldn't guarantee her survival because they had no more drugs. Not only that, but they couldn't feed her: patients now had to provide their own food. A little later the region lost its electricity, so the trams stopped working. This meant Litsa had to walk several miles every day from Kallithea to the hospital to take Maria a can of Red Cross rations, then she walked back home, burning up her own calories in the process.

Miraculously Maria survived. In late September my father got a street vegetable vendor, who no longer had any vegetables to sell, to bring her home in his pushcart. My father wrapped Maria in blankets and he and the vendor pushed the cart for two hours to get her to our house. They were stopped along the way by Germans who wanted to see what was under the blanket.

My experience of illness related to the hardships of the war wasn't limited to my sisters. One of the newcomers to our neighborhood was a young man of eighteen or so called Xaverios Pomidoros, which was especially memorable to me because he was of Italian background and "pomodoro" was the Italian word for a tomato. Like many others he had tuberculosis and his parents, hoping Kallithea had healthier air than central Athens, where they lived, had sent him to stay with his aunt, our neighbor Mrs Perrakis. He never emerged from her house but sat at the window looking out at the street.

Xaverios was extremely handsome and some local girls became infatuated with him. The difference in our ages didn't prevent us from becoming friends. I sat on his windowsill, he inside and I outside, and kept him company. I wasn't afraid of his tuberculosis because my sister Alexandra had it too, but I kept a respectable distance from his breath. I became the go-between entrusted with the delivery of innocent love notes between him and his admirers. It was rather futile because he couldn't go out with them and the girls, despite their professed love, didn't visit him for fear of his illness.

My association with Xaverios was a two-way street: in exchange for my services he told me things about human biology that I found incredible. At first I refused to believe his claims. It seemed to me beyond possibility that my mother and father had engaged in any of the extraordinary behaviors that he so graphically described. But I eventually succumbed to the authority with which he shared his knowledge and in turn I eagerly passed on to my peers what I learned at Xaverios' window. In this manner I contributed to the education of the children of Kallithea.

A few months later Xaverios' parents moved him to a small apartment in Agia Paraskevi, where Alexandra had been sent. The devotion with which they arranged this move, which couldn't have been easy for them, resulted in a sorrow magnified by irony. Because of his relocation, their son was indeed not to die of tuberculosis. One evening a German deserter burst into his apartment and shot him dead. Why? As with the reason for millions of other deaths in that war, no one could say. We heard that the soldier was arrested, tried by a German military tribunal and condemned to death, and that the German commander sent a courier to deliver to Xaverios' father an official invitation to attend the execution. It was to take place at the notorious Kessariani shooting range where Greeks had been massacred.

Mr Pomidoros declined.

German WWII Opel Blitz truck.

CHAPTER 28 : *ALONE*

❝The Germans are going to leave soon," everyone predicted, and by the end of the summer of 1944 there was mounting evidence that this was so.

Shattering thunderclaps periodically shook the air as the invaders blew up installations, evidently so as to leave in their wake nothing that would make the Allies' lives easier. Smoke billowed from the air base at Kalamaki. Soldiers came and went. There was no more lounging on the steps for them, listening to Eleni's music or watching the antics of the neighborhood boys. Most of them busied themselves quietly dismantling the corrugated tin shelters in their truck depot.

The soldiers I knew as Alfred and Arthur disappeared, as did my enemy Willy with the plastered-down hair. Their pensive commander, however, still walked alone every day on our street from Mr Karatzas' house, always at the same time, stooped and silent, hands clasped behind his back, trudging to the compound gate where he was saluted by steel-helmeted guards who no longer smiled at passing girls. Some said that by continuing his solitary walks the commander was deliberately tempting fate, given the increasingly bold activity of the Resistance. This may have been true in view of a report brought to us by the gossipy maid Eleutheria, with whose employers, Mr and Mrs Karatzas, the elegant and aristocratic officer "boarded". It seemed the commander had sat down with them recently for tea, during which he was as courteous as ever but more reticent than usual. At length they saw that his eyes were growing moist, and he looked at them and said in a calm, even voice, *"Deutschland ist kaputt."* ("Germany is broken.") Then he excused himself and retired to his room.

• • •

Although the Germans were still very much among us, as the weeks passed they tended to become less and less visible during the ordinary passage of daily life. One exception to this was when American planes came to bomb us during the daylight hours. Then the Germans' black Opel Blitz trucks scurried out of their compound like a swarm of wasps whose nest had been disturbed. They parked these vehicles under trees throughout Kallithea to hide them from the bombers.

The house of our storytelling neighbor Mr Hadjimihalis, opposite ours, was chosen as one of these protective locations because it had three leafy acacia trees. During every daytime raid over this period of 1944 the same dark Opel Blitz truck with a dent in its left front fender was parked there, always with the same driver, a young soldier barely out of boyhood. While waiting for the raid to end he sat on the truck's running board looking across the street at us. Only a few yards separated us from him when we sat on our front steps or on chairs on the sidewalk to escape the stifling heat inside. We and the German studiously avoiding eye contact. When any of us inadvertently met his gaze, either we or he quickly and somewhat awkwardly turned away without any gesture that might be mistaken for a greeting. A detached formality was very strictly observed on both sides.

At first we called him "the German", pronouncing it derisively with an exaggerated sibilance that mocked his language. But as we got used to him over the course of several air raids and he became a familiar part of our scene, the pleasure of making fun of his language somehow dwindled and we started calling him dispassionately "the German", saying it with no nuance of sneering parody. Eventually, with reluctance and with feelings that no one in our family felt comfortable to discuss, we found ourselves calling him just "the German kid". Which is what he was.

One particularly hot day my grandmother remarked, "He must be thirsty." She looked around for a family response but none was forthcoming. The silence was her answer and we all knew what it meant. He was The Enemy. If anyone saw us offering him a glass of water this simple act of compassion could be misconstrued as giving comfort to our invaders.

So whenever there was an air raid on one of those hot summer days of 1944 the German kid sat there on his running board in the heat, staring at our house, alone.

• • •

The Resistance fighters grew more daring. It wasn't unusual to see them on warm nights walking single file on our street, some with submachine guns brazenly slung across their shoulders, under the noses of the Germans. The young lovers in Kallithea appeared to have been infected by this bravery too. Some sang love songs on the street directly across from the German commander's billet and other German-requisitioned houses. By and by these songs turned into patriotic anthems and the Germans must have been well aware of this. But they ignored them.

Previously, anti-Nazi slogans had sprung up on the walls of houses under cover of night. Now they were painted openly in daylight by small groups of armed fighters. While some wrote the slogans others stood on a corner keeping an eye open for Germans. Many times I joined them and was assigned to help the lookout men keep watch. I performed my task conscientiously and with great patriotic pride. Our house wasn't exempt from the slogans. Like many others it came to resemble a big billboard advertising freedom. And our house was the first thing the Germans over the way saw when they emerged every morning.

• • •

Defiance of the Germans was now expressed not only in slogans and songs but in speeches all over Kallithea. Hit-and-run groups with megaphones appeared out of nowhere, made an anti-German speech that carried far and wide when amplified by the megaphone, and quickly melted away at the sight of a German patrol. I was a great fan of these performances. As soon as I heard a megaphone I dashed off to find the speaker and most of the time I was able to get myself into the middle of the action.

I once followed the sound of a megaphone to Sivitanidios Street near the plateia, outside the milk distributor's shop. A young Resistance fighter with a pistol tucked in his belt was delivering a speech in a stentorian voice. Around him, keeping watch, were about half a dozen of his fellows, some armed. Shopkeepers and many passersby stood on the sidewalk listening. In the forefront of this audience was a large circle of children, including me. Suddenly someone shouted "Germans!" The Resistance men immediately and skillfully vanished into the side streets but the rest of us stood paralyzed. This was unnecessary, for around the corner appeared a lone German soldier who could scarcely have looked less threatening.

{ 262 }

This individual was far from the stereotype of a soldier of Germany or any other country. He was past his prime, around fifty years old, with round steel-rimmed glasses and gray hair. Moreover, he was unarmed, and looked as if he fervently wished he were elsewhere. Though the road was wide, for some reason he was walking down the very middle of it. As he took in the sight of us he moved forward slowly and hesitantly. He carried, of all things, a small worn leather briefcase which he clutched with both hands under his right arm. He looked immensely uneasy and cut a most oddly feeble and un-gainly figure, utterly devoid of any martial characteristic, as though by a cosmic mistake he had been plucked from some accounting office and set down in this street in a uniform that didn't belong to him. He blinked at the hushed crowd that he now found himself confronting and in return we all moved not a hair, but remained in place, eyeballing him with a speechless perplexity that must have mirrored his own dismay. Looking deliberately and artificially for-ward, like a child who suspects that he is in the presence of ghosts but doesn't want to turn his head to check, he proceeded uncertainly up the street as our uninterrupted scrutiny followed his every step. The only sound was his footsteps, as measured as those at a military ceremony such as an execution.

In fact, the feeling had begun to sink in on me that an execution was exactly what we were about to witness, for the Resistance fight-ers must still have been very near, observing this pathetic spectacle with ridicule and amused interest, and if they wished to execute a German soldier before an audience of Greek civilians as a show of their rebellion against the invaders there could not conceivably have been any readier target than this sorry person. He might as well have had a large bull's-eye painted on him. But he was allowed to go on taking his suspenseful and unsteady steps unmolested, and at last he reached the Sivitanidios technical school building which was seemingly his destination, and there he disappeared to the relief of everyone.

The incident would stay with me through the years as a reminder of the vulnerability of the Germans when they were seen in isolation from their military machine. As I grew older I was to wonder whether that timorous and preposterous man treading his nervous way past our watchful congregation ever made it back to whatever humdrum surroundings he had been uprooted from by a quirk of history. I'd wonder, too, whether Arthur, Alfred and the sad-faced commander were reunited with their children, parents, siblings, friends and sweethearts in Germany. I like to think that they mourned the madness beyond their control that had wrenched them from their lives and sent them here, amid bullets and blood, to walk the streets of Kallithea.

• • •

It was fortunate for us that the Resistance fighters had spared that lost-looking soldier, for in 1944 the army of the foundering Third Reich could still strike back with fatal savagery and strength. Newspapers and prominently-displayed posters had warned us that the killing of a single German soldier would have grave consequences for the population. The Germans had demonstrated that this wasn't an idle threat but could involve the execution of dozens of Resistance prisoners or even hundreds of civilians picked at random in the streets. Working-class neighborhoods, especially the ones populated by refugees from Asia Minor, were special targets for reprisals because the Germans saw these areas as dens of communism. The Nazis hated communists on principle, because their slogans about freedom were at odds with the authoritarian ideology of the Nazi Party and the fascist ideology generally. They shared this antipathy toward communism with such right-wing Greeks as they managed to recruit as collaborators. But their focus on perceived leftist districts for reprisals was based not only on politics but also on military considerations, since left-wing groups in Greece were highly active in the Resistance. The Germans were thus only too ready to seize on any supposed provocation as an excuse for a brutal raid on one of these areas. They also tended to use the word "communist" loosely to include anyone who gave them trouble.

There was a pattern to these sweeps of intimidation in poor areas and its shape quickly became widely known as descriptions of raids were circulated by eyewitnesses. The method of these attacks, and the unnerving possibility that one might explode upon one's own neighborhood at any time, became part of the daily consciousness and talk of communities like ours. The word that Greeks used to describe one of these dreaded events was *bloko*.(There are various spellings of it, including *blocco* and *bloka*.)

In a *bloko* dozens of vehicles -- trucks, motorcycles with sidecars, officers' open cars – appeared out of the blue and abruptly surrounded a neighborhood, cordoning it off totally. Armed soldiers in battle dress, both German and Greek collaborationist, spilled out of the trucks and took over the streets. Vehicles with loudspeakers crawled past the houses raucously broadcasting commands for all males between the middle teens and the sixties to congregate in the main square or some other open space. When these had been assembled, masked men, generally thought to be Greek traitors who knew who was who in the neighborhood, chose victims who were bundled into the trucks and taken away not to be seen again. Citizens walking down the street could also be picked up at random. Even a rumor of a German soldier being felled by the Resistance in or near one's neighborhood could cause a hasty mass exodus of the area's teenage and adult males, who fled to relatives and friends in other districts until the report proved to be a false alarm or until the Germans had filled their sacrificial quota.

• • •

As a ten-year-old in 1944 I wasn't in the front rank of danger from these round-ups, but I did experience both a false alarm and a real *bloko* that year. The false alarm came first. Word spread that a German had been shot somewhere in Kallithea. My father thought of going to stay with my aunt Mary in central Athens until the danger of a *bloko* blew over, but decided against it. One day we heard a strange ongoing rumble outside. Investigating, we found that this ocean of noise was the collective sound of many, many walking feet. A multitude of grim-faced men, from the teenage years up, of every description, working-class men and men in suits and ties, men known to our family and unknown, were all making for the tram station to escape before the anticipated *bloko* ensnared them. They were all, as one, moving briskly and with unanimous purpose. There were so numerous that the street couldn't accommodate them all, so they clambered over doorsteps, and we had to step back into our house to avoid the inexorable surge of this mass of human bodies pressing past us as if their lives depended on it, which each of them believed was the case. And yet not one of them was running, perhaps because their male dignity would not permit it, at least in full view of each other.

It turned out presently that the cause of this tide of self-imposed evacuation, the purported killing of a German in Kallithea, was a false rumor, so no *bloko* was immediately launched against our neighborhood, and all those who had fled trickled back when they and their families were convinced that the coast was clear. But the

Germans did strike in Kallithea a few weeks later.

I can't recall what particular Resistance offence triggered this *bloko*, or whether it was even explained to me at the time, or whether my elders themselves knew the precise cause, then or later. I do remember that it was August 28, a day on which the Germans also raided the area of Palea Sfageia near us, a community of those refugees from Asia Minor whom the Nazis regularly harassed.

We were hardly awake when we realized that something was going on outside. I opened the little frosted glass window of our front door and once again the street was filled with a restless caravan of people streaming on their way to the tram station. On the sidewalk right outside our door a gendarme with a rifle shouted that they must turn back but most ignored him. When the hubbub subsided, doors opened and householders stepped out to exchange information, speculations and anxious questions. It transpired that Kallithea was surrounded by German troops and their Greek lackeys, the Security Battalions, to start weeding out "communists" from our area. I'm unsure how they handled the mass flight to the tram station but we heard that some managed to escape. Shortly gendarmes and soldiers went around the neighborhood ordering all males between fourteen and sixty-five to assemble on an open space on Syngrou Street House-to- house searches would be conducted and anyone failing to comply would be shot on the spot. My father was in this age group.

He had no choice but to obey and my sisters and I threw our arms around him in a fever of despair, sure that this was goodbye. He left the house and we watched him until he disappeared up the road.

A pall of misery fell on us. Was this, then, the end for us? With our father gone, what hope was there for us to make our way? The welter of possibilities and confusion that enshrouded us left barely any space within us for a coherent emotion of any kind to crystallize. But uppermost in our breasts must have been the harrowing knowledge that although we still had each other, the loss of our father would nonetheless leave us alone to an extent that was unprecedented in our lives, casting us adrift in a very final sense. But no more than forty minutes or so had gone by when we heard the door open and to our amazement and inexpressible joy this man, who was the center of our lives, stepped in to rejoin us. He told us that on his way to the assembly point he'd been stopped by a gendarme who asked where he was going. When my father told him he replied, "Don't be daft, man. You're too old for them. They want the young ones, the communists. You don't want to go to the slaughter house. Go home, go back to your family."

We spent the rest of that day tensely trying to find out from neighbors what was happening, but everyone was much in the same state of ignorance and dependence on a grapevine of rumor that was vague and ever-varying. Occasionally we heard a burst of machine gun fire or a shot in the distance. As the day faded the neighborhood eventually became quiet and even after all these years I can offer neither myself nor anyone else any certainty as to what took place. Stories went around that men had been executed by machine gun fire and that their bodies had been taken away on trucks, but I never heard any of our neighbors confirm that their family had lost a man during the Kallithea *bloko*. Perhaps the intent of the Nazis on that occasion was not to kill but only to make all in our community realize that as long as they were with us, we lived on the edge of the abyss.

If that was their goal, they succeeded.

CHAPTER 29 : *ENDS AND BEGINNINGS*

On October 11, 1944, I heard the news which had so long been awaited, which at times in recent months had seemed so near that we could almost touch it and taste it, and which had yet taken forever to arrive. The Germans were gone.

It was a Wednesday. I can't recall exactly who told us about the withdrawal; it must have been a neighbor. Word-of-mouth transmission of not only facts but also feelings had never been more electric as they were passed along from person to person. Rumors of an imminent German departure from Athens had been rife. We'd heard that the Reich's forces were on the run everywhere, that the Russian army was in Yugoslavia, poised to trap the Germans unless they moved fast, that it was just a matter of time now, and so on. And yet when the evacuation was confirmed it spread through Kallithea with the impact of an avalanche of surprise. From door to door the tidings went; over the garden walls, from window to window, along the sidewalks and through the streets, with a waving of hands and jubilant exclamations and much nodding of heads. A new light came into the eyes of all, from the very old and doddering to even the very young who couldn't fathom the details but who, with the keen insight of children, grasped as potently as any adult that something momentous had happened. The neighborhood pulsed and throbbed with the realization that at long last the Occupation was over.

From our wardrobe where such things were stored I retrieved two small Greek flags, and taking these with me to wave I went out in the street to join the melee of exultation, relief and prayerful gratitude as people embraced one another, shook each other's hands and shed tears in celebration of our deliverance. Greek flags appeared outside house after house until the street was festooned with them. The rest of that day and deep into the night an exhausting jumble of discussion ensued as to what this meant to Greece as a whole and to our neighborhood and family in particular, as all my elders contributed their varied speculations about the future.

• • •

The revelry was somewhat premature. The Germans were in fact still in Athens, keeping a low profile while preparing to leave. But their retreat was given its full reality the following morning when a group of German soldiers removed the swastika flag from the Acropolis as a throng of Athenians watched. In a gesture of belated respect toward a country they had violated, these troops saluted the shrine of Greece's Unknown Soldier on Syntagma (Constitution) Square, and the bells of Athens pealed out their announcement of the day of freedom. I grabbed my father's binoculars and raced up the wrought-iron steps to the terrace. From the parapet I looked out through the glass across the rooftops of Kallithea to the patient and majestic Acropolis, reposing as it had done for long over two millennia while mighty regimes had arisen and crumbled around it. The spider flag that had fluttered there since April of 1941, casting its shadow over not just Athens but all of Greece, was not to be seen.

Only years later would my mind be equipped to reflect on the fact that the Nazis had endured in Athens for less than an instant in terms of the story of civilization, but to me the black cross had encroached upon us for much of my life and its disappearance was a seismic change. I was but a boy who still ran barefoot through the streets and vacant lots of Kallithea, knowing nothing of the dealings of nations, the causes of war and the powers that were reshaping the world even as my tremulous fingers held the binoculars to my eyes. Still, I knew however dimly, from all I'd been told, from every fragment I'd overheard, from the sum total I'd absorbed in my short life, that the sight on which I gazed represented something vast and immemorial, not just bigger than my small self but dwarfing us all in its silent splendor. I felt, too, its profound connection with the ordeal of my family through long and turbulent years. There welled up in me, from unknown depths, a release of emotion beyond my understanding, far too much for my quavering frame to contain, and it all came pouring and tumbling out of me as I wept.

• • •

The Germans finally pulled out, piling themselves and their supplies on to their trucks, tanks and every means of transport they had. They left Athens via several routes, none of which came through Kallithea, which was on the periphery of their activities despite the compound that had been established in our neighborhood. But my father worked in central Athens and so witnessed much of the collective exit from his office balcony. He later told my sisters and me what he had seen. Work throughout Athens ceased. People occupied every balcony and window. Every building, public and private, displayed the white and blue flag of Greece in different sizes from flagpoles, balcony rails, windows and hands. It was a city of white and blue. In spite of the rejoicing and high emotion that gripped one and all, decorum prevailed, whether because the German convoys moving out of the city were still heavily armed or because of the historic solemnity of the occasion, or perhaps both.

My father said the military caravan had crept along Hippocratous Street with the deliberation and precision we associated with the Germans. His description recalled to my mind that day, a lifetime away, when I'd stood on an Athens street with my sister in the shadow of an imposing parade of German power and seeming invincibility as men and machines rolled by. Because I'd witnessed that impressive and grandiose display, and because we'd lived for so long across the road from an Occupation compound, my father's words easily evoked for me a tangible picture of the scene on which he had looked down from his balcony in the city. He told us of the uncovered backs of the trucks loaded with German soldiers in full battle gear, their rifles and machine guns pointed at the ready toward the crowds who stared impassively at them from streets and flag-bedecked windows and balconies. There was no vociferous demonstration of contempt, no jeering, no cheering. Just the rumble of the departing machineries of war. The Germans had come to Athens with a roar and they were leaving with a murmur. They had spilled blood, caused suffering, spread terror and left behind them a trail of colossal destruction, but as the last of them watched Athens recede from view, his truck lumbering down the road that was to take him and his fellows to their fate, perhaps he knew with a shiver that Hitler's dominion had not succeeded in diminishing by so much as a grain of sand, or even a single atom, the imperishable dignity of Greece.

• • •

The Germans didn't quit Kallithea as they had left Athens. There was no ceremony. Their activity of dismantling had been visible to our community for some time. Over weeks and days trucks had bustled and German commands had been shouted, and then, as if a storm had passed during the night and left behind it a strangely altered morning landscape, the Germans and their supplies and vehicles were gone. Debris occupied the windblown spaces in our neighborhood where the Opel Blitzes and Bedfords and barbed wire and pacing guards had together formed their looming presence among us. Word soon got around that debris wasn't all they had left. Incredibly, they had abandoned weapons and ammunition, I suppose because a speedy exit required them to travel light. This must have been a bonanza for Resistance scavengers, since the rival political groups who controlled these fighters were now on track toward a struggle for power that would usher Greece into a new era of troubles. It was a time of endings but also a time of beginnings.

The news that guns and bullets were lying around our district was also of stupendous interest to boys who'd had enough of watching soldiery from a parentally controlled distance. Every normal boy of my age scoured the area with not a moment's delay. To our enchantment and glee my friends and I found many weapons, some inoperable and some in very good working order, as well as, joy of joys, rifle bullets galore. We built fires to set the bullets off and were hugely entertained to see how they struck all kinds of surfaces in all directions. We competed for the most novel way to explode them, and it must surely count as a miracle that none of us was even injured, let alone killed. For some reason not one of us considered it plausible that the next bullet might choose to pass through his brain. After all, hadn't we just survived a German invasion?

One day my friend Giannis Kostopoulos and I struck gold. Under a patch of weeds on an empty lot we came cross a trophy that would delight any red-blooded boy, a real hand grenade. It looked brand new and was a stick grenade or "potato masher". Its wooden stock, the handle one held before throwing it at a target, was attached to an explosive container resembling a tin can. Neatly packed in the handle was a string with a porcelain bead on its end. You just pulled the string and threw it. The idea of pulling the string and hurling the grenade over a nearby wall, then dropping on our bellies to escape the blast, held a distinct appeal to the healthy boyish imagination but some reservations stirred within us. We finally agreed to detonate the grenade remotely, tying a long string to it and retiring to safety behind the wall before tugging the string. To execute this brilliant plan we lacked one thing, namely string, and we went in search of some. Alas, we returned to make the bitterly disappointed discovery that the grenade was nowhere to be found. We went off indignantly lamenting that things had come to this, when one could not even leave a hand grenade lying around without someone filching it.

To console ourselves we removed the gunpowder from a dozen or so German bullets, stuffed it into one of my father's antique guns of early nineteenth-century vintage, loaded it with a corncob and went up to my terrace. I held the gun tightly and Giannis lit the powder with a match. There was a small swishing sound. The gun flew out of my hands and a cloud of acrid smoke engirdled me. The corncob left the barrel of the ancient gun like a rocket, barely missing Giannis, which was just as well because with that speed and force it would certainly have made a hole in him. Unfortunately some burning wads fell on him, setting his clothes on fire. My skull was ringing like a gong from the concussion and my eardrums were numb so as I stumbled about I heard not a thing but the ringing of a thousand bells. With impeccable survival instinct Giannis stamped and rolled about to extinguish himself. While all this occurred, the alarmed faces of adults of various descriptions appeared at windows and balconies, perhaps wondering whether the Germans had changed their mind and decided to invade us all over again. You would think they would have been grateful that it was just Giannis and me, but no, I was unmercifully lambasted yet again. Our neighbor Miss Poppy screamed that I was going to kill her old mother, who suffered from a heart condition, and so on and so on. Others also commented darkly and once more I had to keep out of sight for several days before it blew over. There was very little justice in the world.

British soldiers captured by Germans in Greece

Bundesarchiv: Bild 146-1973-101-43/photographer: Mayr

CHAPTER 30 : CHESSBOARD

The Germans' abandoned weapons and ammunition eloquently reminded us that they were still part of our lives. For one thing, they hadn't yet left the whole of Greece. They still controlled various Greek islands where they were to hold on until far into 1945.

Moreover, their footprints on the mainland were deep and would take years to erase. In addition to the damage caused by the Allied bombings they'd attracted, the Germans themselves had blown up buildings, port facilities, bridges, radio infrastructures and much else needed to run the country. They wanted the Allies to arrive in a Greece that was chaotic rather than ready to be used as a base from which to attack the retreating German forces. They left intact the large power plant which, when in operation, supplied electricity to the whole plain of Attica, but this omission from their destructive agenda was due only to the quick action of Greek workers and Resistance fighters who barricaded themselves there with enough arms to take a stand. Even so, the Germans would almost certainly have retaken and destroyed the station had they not been pressed for time. Their command had given them an urgent timetable for departure and when they saw it was going to take longer and involve more trouble than they could spare, they shrugged the power plant off and its defenders became the Greek heroes of the day.

As I remember it, though, the plant wasn't able to operate properly, so even after the Germans left there was still no electricity. Also, we had water only on certain days of the week. All the same there was a general consensus that if we were still in a mess, at least we were free. There were no more curfews. We didn't have to look over our shoulders for the Gestapo. Newspapers began appearing with articles that vented all the country's pent-up emotions about the "Huns" and their atrocities. The radio station in Athens was repaired and began transmitting patriotic speeches, folk music, martial tunes and news of the impending collapse of the Reich. Through my father's binoculars I watched a gigantic Greek flag, apparently even bigger than the huge Nazi one, being hoisted on the Acropolis before the delighted eyes of the entire city whose residents assembled on street, balcony, window, roof and hilltop for the occasion. The white and blue unfurling of this banner was greeted by thunderous acclamation as a sea of voices crashed, wave upon wave, against the walls of cathedrals and government buildings and places of business and every structure that could reverberate with sound.

• • •

But a new and angry cloud was moving over Greece. Days after the German evacuation the first British troops arrived in Athens followed by the Greek government in exile, with Prime Minister George Papandreou at its head. During the absence of these politicians from Greece during the years of Occupation, a different political landscape had emerged within the country, so the desire of these people to project an impression of national unanimity, and to speak on behalf of all Greeks, was unsustainable.

The dominant force in Greek political life during the Occupation, namely the Resistance, hadn't been an extension of the pre-war government, nor had it even been a single united entity; the Resistance had rather been an array of factions representing sharply divided and polarized political views. Having invested much energy and human life in fighting for Greece against the Germans, and having built up their organizations and their followings in the process, each of these competitive blocs now inevitably wanted to play a leading role in shaping the future. And they were armed. Tempers were hot and flared into violence. Bullets flew. The British sided with a group that included people

{ 280 }

whom some suspected of having collaborated with the Germans, and there were bitter feelings. The fuse of war was lit afresh, and this time it would be not a united front against foreign invaders but a bloody civil war that would divide and consume Greece for years. We were not yet done with struggle. This fateful trend came to a head on a day that I remember with special clarity because it was December 3, 1944.

It was my birthday. I was eleven years old.

• • •

This milestone in my life was overshadowed by the mass demonstration that took place that day in Syntagma Square, or Constitution Square, in central Athens. It was an auspicious venue, not least because this was where the Germans had given their farewell salute to the shrine of the Unknown Soldier just before leaving the city. That event had closed a chapter of pain in Greece's odyssey; the demonstration now marked the beginning of another. When the Germans left, the multitude had watched them go in restraint and stillness. But today Athens was alive with agitation and clamor.

The British had by this time installed the government in exile in a position of power in Athens. Both this new government and London now had to come to terms with the tensions between the major Resistance groups jockeying for influence in the governance of the country. There was a confusing number of these factions. Among the largest and most important was EAM (an acronym for Ethniko Apeleftherotiko Metopo, or National Liberation Front), a coalition consisting of several organizations, and its armed wing ELAS (Ellinikos Laïkos Apeleftherotikos Stratos, the Greek People's Liberation Army). EAM's politics were leftist and its leading member was the Communist Party.

My Father had this Luger ...

EAM and ELAS were bitterly opposed to the non-communist Resistance group called EDES (Ethnikos Dimokratikos Ellinikos Syndesmos, the National Republican Greek League), whose military wing was EOEA (Ethnikés Omades Ellinon Antarton, the National Groups of Greek Guerrillas).

For a time it looked as if an agreement was being reached for these armed entities to disband and be absorbed into a new national army, but the negotiations fell apart. EAM called on its supporters to demonstrate en masse in Syntagma Square. As thousands surged through the city center, panic descended. Greek policemen opened fire, shooting demonstrators dead. For generations to come historians would struggle to ascertain exactly what happened in the stampede. There is disagreement about the number of fatalities, ranging from fifteen or so to around two dozen or more. But the quantity of blood spilled is less important than the fact that lives were ended needlessly. Dmitri Kessel, a photographer of the American magazine LIFE, was an eyewitness. His pictures appeared a few weeks later in the magazine's Christmas Day edition under the headline *CIVIL WAR BREAKS OUT IN GREECE: Blood flows in ancient streets of Athens as Greek fights Greek.*

According to Kessel, the police shot without provocation. The initial bloodshed enflamed passions further and British soldiers became embroiled. "Spitfires strafed streets," LIFE reported, "and mortar shells left new scars on ancient shrines of beauty... in London, Prime Minister Winston Churchill, although given a vote of confidence on his war record, suffered renewed attacks from British left for his championship of once-exiled Greek conservatives." It did not help that the gendarmes now carrying out the orders of the new government included men who had also served under the Germans. Also, there were those who deeply resented the British for their part in all this, seeing them no longer as liberators but rather as interlopers out to impose their wishes on a country not their own. As word of the Athens disaster swept through our neighborhood, stunning everyone, the realization began to sink in that instead of a new era of stability and reconstruction, yet another nightmare was upon us.

• • •

ELAS was firmly established in Kallithea, and in an effort to dislodge these fighters the British started shelling us. Even the Germans hadn't done this.

The British hit us from the ground and from the air. Once they bombarded us from a ship. Their shells screaming over us shook the air and rattled our walls and eardrums like freight trains speeding through the sky so that I pressed my hands to my ears and cowered as I had in the candle-lit air raid shelter in 1941. The difference was that I was old enough to see the eerie paradox of our attackers this time being the British, whose voice, the BBC, we'd trusted so long, and whose forces we had welcomed as our deliverers. We were caught in the web of Churchill's grand geopolitical designs, expressed in the understanding that he later claimed to have reached with Stalin, the Soviet dictator, dividing the Balkan region into post-war spheres of influence, with Greece falling into the British domain.

Even with Hitler's Reich crumbling, it seemed, we were pawns on a great international chessboard. And in the game of chess, pawns are the most expendable pieces.

• • •

But I was a child of war now, and in the lulls between attacks I nonchalantly resumed my wanderings, gaily disobeying my elders' attempts to keep me behind the supposedly safe walls of our home. I gathered spent ammunition and mortar fragments to add to my collection. I exploded live ammunition for the thrill of it. From behind our neighborhood's many garden walls I peered at skirmishes between the opposing forces, a privileged spectator who was above the fray, although when bullets whistled by me too closely or the firing got too fierce I quickly made for home. This went on day after day.

Once I watched an artillery battle. Three ELAS fighters maneuvered an anti-tank cannon into position on Dimitrakopoulou Street, aiming it at the British lines on Syngrou Avenue. My natural impulse to get a seat as near to the action as possible was restrained by prudence and I stayed a couple of hundred feet away. With intense fascination and the studious attention of a military inspector I observed them loading their gun and firing it at a target invisible to me. They got off three rounds before their foes responded with their own barrage. One of the incoming shells landed next to the cannon and the blast cut off the arm of one of the ELAS fighters. His fellows quickly retreated, carrying him off with them, and their route took them past me. The injured man was covered in blood, his wide eyes skyward. His severed arm was borne by one of his comrades.

• • •

Death was everywhere. Combatants were dying in battle. Non-combatants were being cut down by stray bullets. Since the cemeteries were behind the British lines, the dead were buried wherever a convenient portion of earth could be found. The square called Perivolaki, or Little Orchard, my haunt from early years where I'd once stolen a chocolate, became a burial ground. When the spaces there were full, the disposers of bodies turned to the empty lots over which I'd long so loved to roam. My familiar world became a landscape of makeshift boneyards. The graves were marked by improvised crosses with the names of the dead on scraps of paper, or just with an X. Like our paper money, human life had been devalued.

One day I was sunning myself in the middle of Mantzagriotaki Street. Some children my own age were playing in the same street a block or so away. About a mile distant, also on this street, a British tank was shelling an ELAS barricade. This incongruous scene, combining children's play and deadly battle, had become customary to us by then but as I look back on it now it sums up the strangeness and absurdity of our lives in that beleaguered setting. The other children and I were in the line of fire. Since I was being royally entertained by the explosions and smoke I was annoyed when my sister Litsa called me to come to our table for my daily ration of roasted chickpeas, at that time our only sustenance. I told her I'd be there in a little while because I was watching something interesting, but she insisted that my father wanted me inside right there and then. Grudgingly I went home.

I'd only taken a few steps into the house side when a cry from Litsa called me back. She blurted that something had just flown down the street exactly where I'd been standing. Since my father's command to eat my meal took precedence over all, I ate in haste and rushed out to investigate. What Litsa had seen was a large fragment of an exploded shell. It had bounced at high speed down Mantzagriotaki Street. Scraping the road like a stone skimming a pond, it had plowed through the group of children I'd seen, scalping a girl, Vaso, and cutting off part of the wrist of a boy, Miltos. It then streaked on through the spot where I'd been sunning myself. I found it some two blocks away. It was round and thick, about the diameter of a small tin can, with razor-sharp jagged edges, and weighed about two pounds.

It would have cut me in half.

CHAPTER 31 : NO MAN'S LAND

T he incident with the British shell should have given me a sobering and heightened awareness of my mortality, but it only reinforced my sense that I was somehow invulnerable. I therefore kept to my routine of idling out in the street to enjoy what warmth the winter sun provided to fortify me against the cold of our home. As always, stray bullets zoomed above me before embedding themselves in walls or falling to the ground, but with an indifference that astounds me when I look back on it, I mostly ignored them.

One day the drone of an aircraft made me look up. It was a Royal Air Force DC3 Dakota flying so low over our neighborhood that I could see the pilot quite clearly. From an open hatch it was dispersing upon our streets, gardens, rooftops and terraces a snowstorm of pieces of paper. They swirled and billowed among the air currents before drifting down in a blizzard. The plane passed over quickly and was soon out of view. I darted to catch some of the floating papers but a gust sprang up and flung them away in a tumbling cloud. They swept and spiraled beyond the reach of my grasping fingers as I gave chase. I dashed and leaped in pursuit but as soon as I stretched to grab them they danced tantalizingly and ever farther away. I raced after them for blocks and the more I exerted myself to seize one the more they retreated from my frustrated lunges, as unattainable as the moon that I'd tried so hard to touch as a small child.

Eventually I managed to snatch one from the ground before it was caught in another updraft. I was now a block or so from the main thoroughfare of Syngrou Avenue and within sight of the British tanks positioned there. Out of breath, I studied the paper. It was a leaflet warning that all civilians must evacuate Kallithea within twenty-four hours, after which time our area would be considered enemy territory and bombed at will. It was in Greek and at the bottom in bold print was the name of General Ronald Scobie, commander of the British forces.

• • •

I realized the urgency of it and holding the leaflet tightly I started for home. My belief in my immunity from destruction was at last evaporating and I hugged the walls, hearing the odd bullet around me as I made my way. Halfway home a lady hailed me from her doorstep and asked if the paper in my hand was from the plane.

"Yes, Missus."

"May I read it, please?"

I handed it over and as she glanced through it her face drained. But her first concern was for me; the marks of my starvation must have been conspicuous, for she asked, "Would you like a slice of bread?"

Bread! I hadn't tasted or even seen it for many months. The prospect of eating a piece of it now should have been irresistible to me. However, the thought flashed through my mind that this kind woman had mistaken me for a street urchin, a beggar, and something in me recoiled from this with shame. I had a home, after all, and had absorbed from my mother the powerful pride that she had always felt in her home and in the independence and self-sufficiency of our family, so although it was perverse and not at all rational in view of my clear realization that I was malnourished, I replied, "No thanks, Missus. I'm not hungry." I took back the leaflet and ran the rest of the way home, cursing myself with each step for refusing that slice of bread. The image of this forfeited treat would remain with me for months as I revisited it repeatedly and tormented myself by imagining its texture and taste in vivid, palpable and mouth-watering detail.

• • •

After reading the leaflet my father hastened to tell the neighbors and before long the area was abuzz. People wondered how such a thing could be happening. Was it really possible that the British, to whom who we had looked as our saviors from the Nazi scourge, were now about to launch a military offensive against the homes of civilians? How could all the people leave their houses at such short notice and evacuate Kallithea? Where could they go? For many, their only friends and relatives lived miles away. And with all that everyone had recently been through and was still undergoing, who could say whether any friend or relative was in a position to take them in? And in any case, how were people to get safely to these supposed places of refuge in a terrain that was clearly a battleground? What was in the mind of general Scobie to make him inflict such an upheaval upon mothers, children, the ill, the starved and the elderly, in a country where he was at most a visitor? How could such action by the British be regarded as just, or even as responsible? How thin was the line between the role of a liberator and the role of an invader establishing a new occupation regime under the guise of an unelected government whose authority General Scobie wished to impose on us through the barrels of British guns?

• • •

In the days following the catastrophe on Syntagma Square the British may still have enjoyed some benefit of the doubt but this had withered steadily as they stormed the suburbs. By raising a thicket of moral questions that weren't easy to answer for anyone sympathetic to the British, General Scobie put a torch to the goodwill with which many of the people of Athens had initially received him.

{ 289 }

Ilias and Hippocrates Syrakos, our good friends and neighbors and members of our assembly of dining room generals, offered our family an emergency solution. Ilias was the manager of a large textile factory on Mantzagriotaki Street. It occupied two blocks and bordered Syngrou Avenue, which was held by the British. It was now idle and locked but Ilias had a key and suggested we hunker down there. There was a lot of cloth in storage so we'd have bedding.

After a brief family council it was decided that my grandmother, Maria, Litsa and I would take shelter at the factory until it was safe to return home. Alexandra was too ill to move. Although she didn't complain she was terribly weak, bedridden and clearly in agony. My father stayed with her. It was late afternoon when we left the house after a farewell to my father and Alexandra which we all realized might be our last. We were now in the hands of Hippocrates, who was a Resistance member and also, according to some later reports, a participant in the political activity of the organization EAM. He made us take with us the biggest white cloths we could find, waving these as we made our cautious way to the factory. I tied mine on a short stick.

• • •

We went down Iphigenias Street toward Syngrou Avenue and the British lines, past the site of the former German truck depot. Behind sandbags on the corner of Saphous and Iphigenias Streets a group of ELAS fighters were firing at the British with a light machine gun. We took cover against a wall directly behind them. Hippocrates left us briefly to speak with the ELAS men who agreed to stop firing until we reached the factory.

We could only hope the British would do the same. Since the streets were laid out in a grid of straight lines, and one end of Iphigenias Street was held by ELAS fighters and the other by the British, we were utterly exposed as we proceeded. It was like walking through a mile-long shooting gallery. If anyone on either side started shooting we would be cut down in seconds. We passed the ELAS fighters and walked slowly in the middle of the street, five abreast, waving our white cloths, which for some reason we all held in our left hands. Were the British behind their barricades able to see Yaya, Litsa, Hippocrates, Maria and me clearly enough through their binoculars? Would they understand that we were harmless refugees?

We walked with excruciating slowness because my grandmother waddled ponderously and painfully on her arthritic legs. It was only with the greatest difficulty that I held in check the almost overwhelming urge to break into a run. Sporadic explosions and bursts of machine gun fire came to us from other streets, reminding us with every footstep that we in a battle zone as precarious as a minefield. We walked silently except for Yaya's stream of muttered invocations of every saint she could think of as crossed herself constantly with her right hand.

We had made it about halfway to the factory when, for what reason I don't know, someone on the British side fired and a hail of bullets flew. As far as I remember the Resistance fighters kept their promise and didn't respond and the shots came only from the British. We scrambled for the cover of the nearest wall but Yaya tripped and fell. The rest of us, huddling under partial cover, looked back to see my grandmother lying in a helpless heap in the road. Hippocrates wrenched a white cloth from one of us, I cannot recall from whom, and holding one cloth in each hand he strode to my grandmother. Planting his feet apart, he raised his two white pennants aloft so that his body formed a big X. Standing thus protectively above the old lady, he resembled, I would realize in later years, the great artist Leonardo da Vinci's drawing of Vitruvian Man, which has come to be lodged in the imagination of the world as a universal symbol of humanity. But at the time, seen through my eleven-year-old eyes, he was nothing as exalted as this but more like a bear rearing over its family with primeval instinct. He shouted at the British, "Shoot, you cowards! Come on, shoot me first! Not an innocent woman!" This exclamation was only for the venting of his own fury because the British could not possibly have heard him; they must have been half a mile away. What mattered is that they didn't shoot. Hippocrates helped Yaya to her unsteady feet and we all warily resumed our trek through No Man's Land.

• • •

When we finally entered the factory, a drab two-story building, it turned out that others had also sought refuge there. My sisters settled down with Yaya while I accompanied Hippocrates as he looked around. We found that a wall facing Syngrou Avenue had been shelled and had a large hole in it, big enough for a man to walk through. Hippocrates poked his head out to peep at the British barricades and I followed suit. He pulled me back roughly as a burst of automatic fired raked the wall. Continuing our exploration, we came across an immense room in the center of the building, piled high with sacks which we arranged as well as we could. There we huddled until night came, and we slept.

• • •

No bombardment awakened me during the night; morning found me stiff but grateful to be alive. Some of the refugees had ventured out and reported that the ELAS fighters had decided to withdraw and leave Kallithea to the British. But we didn't leave immediately as we couldn't count on rumor. There was, moreover, an advantage to staying where we were a little longer because some of the fugitives had made a fire and were cooking soup, real bean soup with tomato sauce and real olive oil. Its hearty, bubbling spectacle and mouth-watering aroma, which I hadn't known for years, entranced me and we were all served generous portions; indeed I was allowed to gorge myself. In the early afternoon Hippocrates decided it was safe to leave and we set off for home. There were no gunshots or explosions. The ELAS fighters were gone. We felt safe for the first time in many months, but uncertainty about my father and Alexandra accompanied us all the way until we stepped into our house to find that they were unharmed.

• • •

Kallithea was once again an enclave of foreign troops, as it had been in the days of the Germans. This time the uniforms were British and the vehicles were American jeeps and GMC, Dodge and Chevrolet military trucks, all painted olive-drab in contrast to the black German counterparts they had replaced. But to me much had not changed. We were almost as hungry as we'd been under the Germans. In addition, the British had requisitioned my school for their soldiers, depriving us of learning for two months until they found a replacement. When we got it back the school was without electricity or water. I had to carry my own water to school in a glass bottle that I guarded with my life. The Germans were gone but we were still at war. And I came to understand that my long, tense and hazardous walk with Yaya, Litsa, Maria and Hippocrates had been just the beginning of a longer passage of fire for us all. For not just one street nor one neighborhood nor even one city but all of Greece had now become a No Man's Land. But I was eleven now, and old enough to know, however dimly, that all things men do must come to an end, and that one day we would be free.

EPILOGUE: OTHER ROADS, DIFFERENT JOURNEYS

In the post-war trials at Nuremberg, Germany, military officers of the Hitler era were prosecuted for crimes against humanity including complicity in slave labor, plunder, wanton destruction and other atrocities against civilians. In one of these trials the prisoners in the dock included Luftwaffe General Helmuth Felmy, who had carried out Hitler's commands in Greece.

The prosecutor, Telford Taylor, told the court: "Lidice, the small Czech village which the Germans leveled to the ground in 1942, stands today as a symbol of German savagery. In Greece there are a thousand Lidices, their names unknown and their inhabitants forgotten by a world too busy and too cynical to remember." Taylor believed that the world's media had already glossed over what Greece had suffered.

The year was 1948.

• • •

Greece, Taylor told the judges at Nuremberg, was a country of many small villages of five hundred to a thousand people, with mud houses that had been occupied for centuries. These had been among the places razed by German troops under Felmy's command on just one rampage in December, 1943. The carnage had lasted for eight days "before their senseless bestiality had been satiated. Fourteen villages were completely destroyed and their male inhabitants shot." Over five hundred people from one village alone, Kalavryta, were executed.

The prosecution described other atrocities, a long and grisly list of them, drawing on the Germans' own records, which they'd kept meticulously as if they were proud of their clerical correctness in memorializing their works of horror. Taylor noted that the Balkans had been an Achilles heel to German aggression, and a mystery to the Reich. "The generals were never able to understand why – but strong, independent peoples accustomed to hardship, inured to suffering, and born to freedom, can no more be broken by tyranny than a diamond scratched by a sword." Taylor took the words at the end of this sentence from a novel of the time called *Guerrilla*. Its Irish author, Lord Dunsany, had been Professor of English at Athens University in 1940 when he was evacuated.

• • •

General Felmy was sentenced to fifteen years imprisonment. A clemency board later reduced his sentence and his early release was approved in 1951. He died in Darmstadt, Germany, in 1965.

• • •

Felmy and his cohorts weren't the only ones who found themselves embarking on other roads and different journeys after the war. For some half a dozen years my family and everyone we knew toiled to rebuild our shattered lives as civil war engulfed us.

After the British under General Scobie seized Athens, the ELAS fighters took to the mountains again, just as they had in the time of the Axis invasion. Their earlier sacrifice in blood and lives, when they'd bravely stood against Mussolini and Hitler, was discounted now. What mattered was that they didn't hold the political views that Britain wished to promote in the game of international manipulation. Heroic Greek patriots became persona non grata as right-wing organizations were strengthened by the British, who in turn were supported by a wealthy and powerful America.

My family and neighborhood soon realized we'd entered an era that was to be dominated by American influence. A symbol of this was the canned food with which we now became familiar: it came from the American military. And when we managed to go to the movies once in a while we saw very clearly how it was going to be. The massively funded Anglo-American media, especially the vast resources of Hollywood and the British film industry, was busily manufacturing an entertaining version of history in which the war was portrayed as largely an American and British experience. Europe simply happened to be the quaint and accidental backdrop for Anglo-American heroics. There was occasional mention of Resistance movements in France, Italy and even Germany. The conspicuous absence of Greece from these swashbuckling accounts raised many a sardonic Greek smile.

When I look back to my memories of those years, amplified by later reading and by talking with others who remembered the war, I'm awed by how Greeks alone resisted the Axis at a time when there were no Americans in sight, when Britain was staggering under Hitler's blows, and when other countries in Europe were under the German heel.

Greece's stand paved the way and created the strategic window for the Soviet Union's eventual repulsion of the Germans from the east, ultimately enabling the Reich to be caught in a vise as Britain, America and their allies closed in from the west. But a flood of ingenious storytelling in postwar books, magazines and films now poured out of Britain and America's media factories, telling a different tale that shapes the world's understanding to this day.

Great is the power of those who create myths.

• • •

There were, to be sure, some satisfying moments after the war, such as when Italy finally acknowledged that the submarine "of unknown nationality" that had sunk the Greek vessel Elli had in fact been Italian. Greece received a cruiser from Italy in reparation.

But even when peace of a sort came, Greece remained a troubled country. The legacy of the British political intervention wasn't the democracy for which Greeks had longed and hoped and suffered during the Occupation, but rather its opposite: dictatorship. The right-wingers, whom the British had empowered, at last openly showed their contempt for democracy by seizing power in a coup. A military junta took over the government.

Greece, the cradle of democracy, the resister of fascism, was ruled by a uniformed dictatorship from 1967 to 1974.

• • •

Greece's King George II, to whose arms I'd so embarrassingly and disrespectfully refused to go at the Olympic Stadium, and who was returned to Greece by the British after the war, died of arterial illness in Athens in 1947. He was succeeded by his brother Prince Paul, who reigned until his death from cancer in 1964. Paul's son, Constantine II, reigned from then until the military junta abolished the Greek monarchy in 1973. When this book was being prepared for publication he was still living in exile, his titles unrecognized by the government of Greece. But because of the close familial connections among the royal houses of Europe, he remained a recognized prince in the Kingdom of Denmark.

• • •

The politician whom the British installed as prime minister in 1944, Georgios Papandreou, served only until the following year, but he became prime minister again twice in later years. He died in 1968. His son and grandson both became prime ministers of Greece. The son, Andreas, also held the office twice, his second term ending in 1996, the year of his death. The grandson, Georgios, became prime minister in 2009. He resigned in 2011 amid Greece's national debt crisis.

• • •

General Scobie, who oversaw Britain's military support for the right wing at the end of the war, and whose troops fired on my grandmother, Litsa, Maria, our neighbor Hippocrates and me, retired from the military in 1947. He died in 1969, full of honors from his wartime service, including a knighthood. In 1975 his exploits were the subject of a book called *Scobie, Hero of Greece: the British campaign 1944-5*, by Henry Maule.

Winston Churchill was voted out of office in 1945. He returned for another term as Britain's prime minister in1951, serving until 1955. He died in 1965. In 2008 a public opinion poll in Britain revealed that twenty-three percent of the participants thought he was a fictional character.

• • •

On a spring evening on the plateia of Leonidion in 1942, when the village lawyer Nikos Mavrakis captivated us with his visions of the twenty-first century, Alexandra told me that I might live to see the year 2000. She was right. But she didn't make it. My lovely sister died of the effects of tuberculosis in April, 1947. She was twenty-three. Her fiancé, Nikos Symeonidis, who as a boy had shared a basement shelter with us during the air raids, tenderly nursed her until the end. When he married years later, his wife agreed that Alexandra's picture would always remain on their living room wall.

Nikos Mavrakis joined the Greek Resistance. In 1944 he and a group of fighters were ambushed outside Leonidion by a German unit. Most of his unit escaped. Nikos didn't. He lies buried in those hills to this day.

After the war we also heard again of Sonia Salahas, the Russian wife of Leonidion's telegrapher. In August of 1944, the Germans sent a punitive expedition to Leonidion to deal with the Resistance. They engaged in an orgy of killing. Arresting a teenage boy who'd hidden a pair of military boots, they accused him of being in the Resistance and condemned him to death. Mrs Salahas, whose curves had kindled such romantic feelings in my imagination, could speak German and she went to the German commander and begged for mercy for their teenage prisoner. They sent her away. The boy was shot.

In the year of Alexandra's death, Maria married a Greek American and they moved to the United States. When this book was being prepared she was in a home for Alzheimer's patients in California, finally at peace with herself in a private world where the turbulence of our time could no longer hurt her.

In 1954 my sister Litsa married Alekos Moustakis, who'd been my

Scout Leader, my mentor and later my best friend. Litsa was thirteen when we lost our mother. She was my surrogate mother to me and raised me, assuming household responsibilities that no child should have to bear. When this book was being produced she was living in greater Athens with her daughter and family. She was eighty-three.

• • •

Lambis Konstantinidis, whose life I endangered when I so unthinkingly turned the lights on and off at his family's seaside villa during the blackout, became a successful professional man in New York City. In 1988 I visited him and his wife Diana after his sixty-fifth birthday. At a Greek celebration two years later he died dancing, affirming his zest for life in the timeless way of Zorba, the quintessential Greek created by the great writer Nikos Kazantzakis.

The brothers Ilias, Hippocrates and Nikos Syrakos, who were part of my father's war cabinet of dining room generals, left our neighborhood after the war. Hippocrates, who took us to the textile factory to escape the threatened British bombardment, and who so courageously went to our Yaya's help when she lay in the road exposed to the British guns, was imprisoned for a long time by the post-war government, like many others whose political beliefs didn't meet with British approval. Eventually he was released on condition that he left Greece forever.

Hippocrates married one of our Kallithea neighbors and settled in Zurich, Switzerland, working as an engineer. We corresponded, especially during the years of the Greek military dictatorship, and he kept me informed of efforts outside Greece to oppose that regime. Despite the great difference in our ages, a quarter of a century or so, we were firm friends. Over the years we met in Switzerland and Britain. He was at length able to return to Greece after the government granted amnesty to all political dissenters.

The last time I saw him was in 1996, in Athens. His wife led me to his bed. He'd had a stroke and had lost all contact with the outside world. He moaned softly to himself. "He does not respond to anyone or anything," his wife told me. She squeezed his hand. "Vagelis is here from London to visit you." The moaning stopped and he smiled faintly for a few seconds. Then he was gone again.

But sometimes a few seconds are all you need.

• • •

We learned that my cousin Achileas Loizos, whose body was washed up on the shore of Turkey after he was shot by Germans while trying to escape from Greece in a dinghy, was buried near the beach where he was found. I gather the site of his grave is today a parking lot covered by asphalt.

The kiosk at the plateia called Perivolaki, Little Orchard, from which I stole a chocolate, causing my mother to march me in shame to confess my crime, survived the war. In the early nineteen-forties its management passed from the gentleman who owned to it to his young daughter, Militsa. When this book was in production, a decade into the twenty-first century, she was still at work there.

Colonel Davakis, the hero of Pindus who held me on his lap in the hospital, was captured by the Italians in December of 1942. They put him on an Axis ship to be taken to a prison camp in Italy. The ship was torpedoed by a British submarine and he drowned. In Kallithea the Dimitros Street of my childhood was renamed Davaki Street in his memory, and Plateia Dimitros (Dimitros Square) became Plateia Davaki. A statue of Davakis stands there today, an outstretched hand pointing to the distant Pindus Mountains. The achievement of men like Davakis and those who fought with him was decisive for the war. After the many months in which the Greeks kept the Italians in constant retreat, Hitler at last had to intervene to save Mussolini, and this made him delay his invasion of the Soviet Union from May to June. Because of this, the momentum of Hitler's armies ground to a frozen halt outside Moscow in December, 1941, driving them back to a defeat which in turn critically affected the course of the war. If not for the struggle of the Greek people, Hitler would in all probability have taken Moscow in October, before the onset of the Russian winter, and the outcome of World War Two would have been different. Greece's heroism thus gave the free world its first victory over fascism in those dark days.

Perhaps nothing sums this heroism up as well as the story of the women of Pindus. As 1940 drew to a close, our soldiers high in the mountains were running out of ammunition and there weren't enough packing animals or men to transport new supplies. As they'd done previously, the women of the villages of Epirus left their homes to come to the rescue. In the dead of winter, dragging their long skirts through the wet snow, they carried the heavy boxes on their backs to their men on the battleground. If you go to the village of Aspraggeloi today you can see a statue called *The Woman of Pindus*. It depicts a woman in Epirus costume, her shoulders bearing her burden for the troops. It is evocative, but it can't call forth more emotion than was felt by the beleaguered soldiers to whom those remarkable women made their journeys. Nor can it match the pride that reports of their actions brought into the homes of the Athens and Kallithea of my childhood, when the news of it was fresh from the doing, and when we Greeks so needed to be reminded of the great people we had always been, and still were.

• • •

And what of me?

In 1953, at nineteen, with no means to obtain higher education, I became a merchant seaman and set off on my own long journey into the years.

In 1955, with just twenty dollars in my pocket, I arrived in the United States where Maria, thanks to her marriage to an American, was able to sponsor me. (Like many immigrants, I found that my American papers changed the spelling of my last name; my original Greek name Loizos became the Louizos that it remains today.) I worked as a bartender, a janitor, a house painter, an auto mechanic. I married, raised a family, studied, earned a degree and became a teacher.

My grandmother, my Yaya, who had played so great a role in my survival, called my name on her deathbed in 1958. I was on the other side of the Atlantic when she died at eighty-three, but I know that at the last she was proud of me and loved me.

She always had.

Echoes of the war continued to find me in my wanderings over the decades. In 1970, impressed by a counterman's faultless Greek at Corti Brothers, an Italian delicatessen in Sacramento, California, I asked: "Are you Greek?" His reply: "I'm Italian. When I escaped from the Germans in 1943 a Greek family gave me shelter. I fell in love with their daughter and married her."

In America I met Marinos George, who told me how Major Kostakis had made him recite the Lord's Prayer as a punishment for cursing, and how the Germans had humiliated the Italian soldiers in the

Tripoli taverna. Marinos and I cleaned bars at night in Marysville, California, he to feed his family, I to put myself through college. He grew carnations which he hawked in the bars, calling in his broken English, "Flowers for the mens! Flowers for the mens!" In the bars and at the school where he worked as custodian he was called George the Flower Man. To me he was a witness to history and my dear friend. He died in Marysville on April 16, 2009, having survived not only Mussolini's bullets and bombs but also the hard personal voyage that followed. He was ninety-three.

In 1959 my father retired, aged sixty-three. A year later, before he could embark on a planned trip to America to see me and his first grandchildren, he had a stroke. His fine mind, whose clarity and control had seen us through the war, was irreparably damaged. He slipped into a world of shadows from the past that no one else could see. He died a few months later.

Today his old wartime workplace, The Barracks, is forgotten. The grounds on which it stood are the home of a new military hospital and other buildings neighboring the Megaron Mousikis (Mansion of Music), a vast concert hall where musicians come from all over the world to perform. Interwoven with their music are the ghostly footsteps of the thousands of Italian prisoners of war for whom my father was responsible.

• • •

I became a traveler. If my childhood gave me anything, it was a sense of history. I longed to see where the history of our world had been made. I hoped this would help me understand why the world was as it was and how it could be made better.

I retraced the routes of the explorers Marco Polo, Magellan, Captain

Cook and others. I traveled the Sahara on a camel. I sailed the Amazon River and climbed the Andes Mountains of South America. I've known the Sierra Madre crags of Mexico and the deep jungles of Brazil. I've visited palaces from Berlin, Moscow and Beijing to Hu , Vietnam, where great monarchs once lived; I've stood in sorrow at the sites of the battles they brought about. I've seen the graves left by countless wars. At the Livadia Palace near Yalta, in Ukraine, I stood before a table where Stalin and Churchill decided and divided control of the destinies of millions to their respective advantages, as part of the spoils of war.

I've been lucky to meet an enormous variety of people, from those in high places to the most wretched. In Bolivia I sat with peasants, chewing the coca leaves they use to cheat their hunger just as I did with nettles and carobs during the Occupation. I sang with them in praise of love, justice and freedom. Together we lamented pain, anguish and oppression. We prayed for a better world.

The image of the Luger Parabellum pistol has remained fixed in my mind over all the years of my life. My father tried to control it by locking it away. To him it may have symbolized all the might of Germany, but although I myself looked into the black barrel of a Luger that night when I felt the breath of eternal darkness upon me, distance and time inevitably change one's thoughts. With the years the Luger came to signify for me the greatest mistake that Hitler and his minions made, which was to underestimate the powers in humanity that are not made of steel and not designed by arms manufacturers. It was a mistake that cost Germany the war.

But I was not the only one on whose imagination the Luger came to be so deeply engraved. It has continued to be manufactured into the twenty-first century and World War Two specimens are collectors' items that fetch enormous prices. More than ever it is today an almost mythic symbol of Hitler's Germany that exercises a macabre fascination for those who choose to steep themselves in the lore of the Third Reich. I wonder how many people know that the name of the Luger Parabellum comes from an old Latin saying: *Si vis pacem, para bellum*: "If you want peace, prepare for war."

This must be one of the saddest comments ever made.

As a teacher I've spent a good deal of my life trying to share such knowledge as I've managed to accumulate. I have sometimes seen myself as a Don Quixote tilting at windmills, for the evidence that we learn from history is scant.

But we must hope. Without hope, we have nothing. Perhaps hope, more than anything else, enabled us in Greece to survive that era of agony.

Every few years I go back to Kallithea, where I learned to taste life. There is almost nothing left from those days now. Yet it always comes flooding back to me, because I remember. And in honor of all those who shared that time and that place with me, I leave this testament.

I asked my mother why the sirens wailed. She didn't answer me, and I understand now that it was because, in the fullest sense of my question, she didn't know how to.

Do you?

My Father had this Luger ...

Mama

Made in the USA
San Bernardino, CA
19 February 2013